Serbians in Michigan

DISCOVERING THE PEOPLES OF MICHIGAN

Russell M. Magnaghi, *Series Editor*
Arthur W. Helweg and Linwood H. Cousins, *Founding Editors*

Ethnicity in Michigan: Issues and People
Jack Glazier and Arthur W. Helweg

African Americans in Michigan
Lewis Walker, Benjamin C. Wilson, Linwood H. Cousins

Albanians in Michigan
Frances Trix

Amish in Michigan
Gertrude Enders Huntington

Arab Americans in Michigan
Rosina J. Hassoun

Asian Indians in Michigan
Arthur W. Helweg

Belgians in Michigan
Bernard A. Cook

Chaldeans in Michigan
Mary C. Sengstock

Copts in Michigan
Eliot Dickinson

Cornish in Michigan
Russell M. Magnaghi

Danes and Icelanders in Michigan
Howard L. Nicholson, Anders J. Gillis, and Russell M. Magnaghi

Dutch in Michigan
Larry ten Harmsel

Finland-Swedes in Michigan
Mika Roinila

Finns in Michigan
Gary Kaunonen

French Canadians in Michigan
John P. DuLong

Germans in Michigan
Jeremy W. Kilar

Greeks in Michigan
Stavros K. Frangos

Haitians in Michigan
Michael Largey

Hmong Americans in Michigan
Martha Aladjem Bloomfield

Hungarians in Michigan
Éva V. Huseby-Darvas

Irish in Michigan
Seamus P. Metress and Eileen K. Metress

Italians in Michigan
Russell M. Magnaghi

Jews in Michigan
Judith Levin Cantor

Latinos in Michigan
David A. Badillo

Latvians in Michigan
Silvija D. Meja

Lithuanians in Michigan
Marius K. Grazulis

Maltese in Michigan
Joseph M. Lubig

Mexicans and Mexican Americans in Michigan
Rudolph Valier Alvarado and Sonya Yvette Alvarado

Norwegians in Michigan
Clifford Davidson

Poles in Michigan
Dennis Badaczewski

Scandinavians in Michigan
Jeffrey W. Hancks

Scots in Michigan
Alan T. Forrester

Serbians in Michigan
Paul Lubotina

South Slavs in Michigan
Daniel Cetinich

Swedes in Michigan
Rebecca J. Mead

Yankees in Michigan
Brian C. Wilson

Discovering the Peoples of Michigan is a series of publications examining the state's rich multicultural heritage. The series makes available an interesting, affordable, and varied collection of books that enables students and educated lay readers to explore Michigan's ethnic dynamics. A knowledge of the state's rapidly changing multicultural history has far-reaching implications for human relations, education, public policy, and planning. We believe that Discovering the Peoples of Michigan will enhance understanding of the unique contributions that diverse and often unrecognized communities have made to Michigan's history and culture.

Serbians in Michigan

Paul Lubotina

Michigan State University Press

East Lansing

Michigan State University Press
East Lansing, Michigan 48823-5245

Printed and bound in the United States of America.

20 19 18 17 16 15 14 1 2 3 4 5 6 7 8 9 10

LIBRARY OF CONGRESS CONTROL NUMBER: 2014931990
ISBN 978-1-61186-141-9 (pbk.)
ISBN 978-1-60917-427-9 (ebook: PDF)
ISBN 978-1-62895-026-7 (ebook: ePub)
ISBN 978-1-62896-026-6 (ebook: Kindle)

Interior design by Charlie Sharp, Sharp Des!gns, Lansing, MI
Cover design by Ariana Grabec-Dingman
Cover image is of Serbian folk dancing at Detroit's Masonic Temple, 1960 (photo ID 79612) and is used with permission of Walter P. Reuther Library, Archives of Labor and Urban Affairs, Wayne State University.

Michigan State University Press is a member of the Green Press Initiative and is committed to developing and encouraging ecologically responsible publishing practices. For more information about the Green Press Initiative and the use of recycled paper in book publishing, please visit *www.greenpressinitiative.org*.

Visit Michigan State University Press at *www.msupress.org*

I would like to thank my wife, Michelle, and daughters Olivia and Natalie for their support while writing this book. I also want to thank Markku Mikkola and his family, who also helped in the early stages of research into Slavic cultures. Furthermore, I wish to dedicate this work to the memory of my family members who did not live to see the completion of this project. These include Peter, Josephine, and Elizabeth Lubotina, Arno, Jenny, and Fred Pesola, along with my nephew, Ryan Dezurik.

Contents

Introduction

The story of Serbian immigrants in Michigan is one of integration and ethnic retention. The core of Serbian identity derives from their adherence to the Orthodox faith. While Serbs, Croats, Slovenes, and Bosnians all descend from the same ancient peoples, their modern counterparts have embraced Orthodoxy, Catholicism, and Islam, which has helped to separate the populations into distinct ethnic groups. For Serbs, their religious beliefs defined and helped to preserve their ethnic identity through centuries of occupation by the Ottoman Empire. During that period, three key elements emerged that defined Serbian ethnic identity. These included Orthodoxy (*Svetosavlje*) and kinship (*kumstvo*), along with nationalistic ideas maintained through the repeated sharing of epic folk stories that commemorated important events such as the 1389 Battle of Kosovo, which led to Ottoman domination and the 1804 Serbian Revolt that finally paved the way to independence. Serbian children memorized and recited or sang the stories, along with their catechism lessons as they grew into adulthood. When they too had children, the process continued, even to this day. In this method, Serbian heritage has been preserved through several generations of Americanization.

That did not mean that Serbian immigrants were without any internal disputes among the members. The strongest and longest-lasting conflict erupted between political liberals and conservatives in communities around

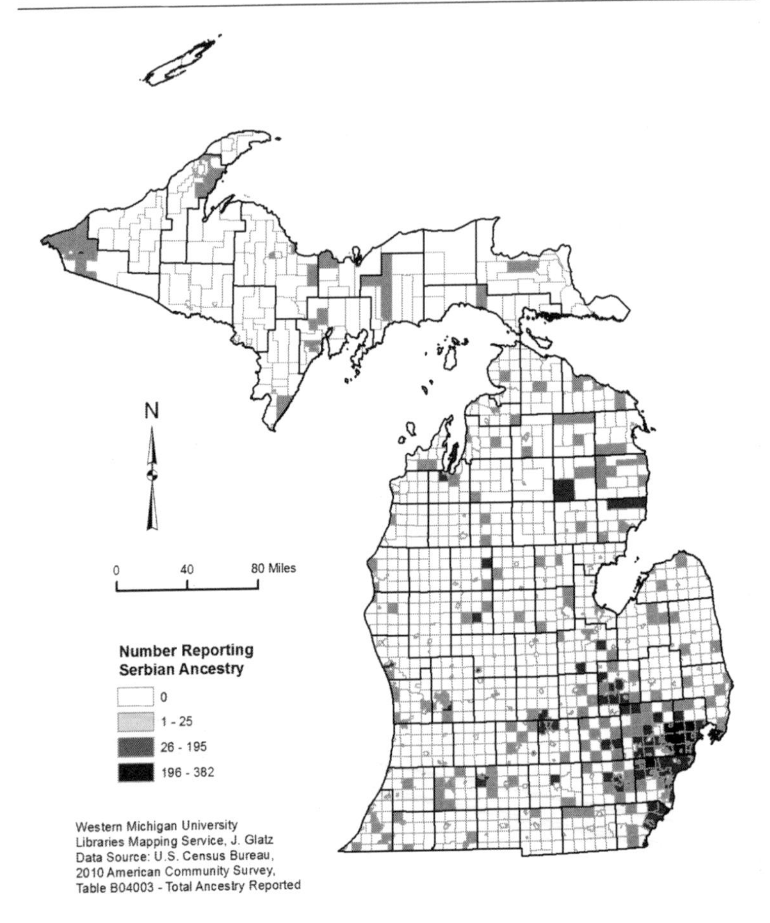

the United States, including Detroit. However, the line between liberals and conservatives blurred over time. In the early twentieth century, there was a distinct difference between the socialists and communists on the left and those who adopted American political traditions of supporting the Republican or Democratic parties. By the 1950s, that line had blurred as a communist revolution in Yugoslavia resulted in large numbers of ardent anticommunists coming to America. Their arrival heralded a new round of liberal and conservative debates, only the conservatives of the early twentieth century were labeled liberals by the newly arrived immigrants. In 1963, the conflict resulted in a religious schism between the two groups that would last for nearly thirty years. The Serbian Orthodox Church resolved the differences in 1991, which brought a reunification of Serbian American communities. In so doing, the church continued its role of uniting Serbian people, even in America.

However, other issues such as interethnic marriage, religious disputes, or a myriad of other personal choices have created a situation where people of Serbian heritage have lost contact with the greater Serbian American community. This book was written to give anyone with an interest in Serbian immigrant history a broad perspective of the Serbian American experience in Michigan. It also includes information on immigrant participation in national organizations and interactions with other enclaves around the United States. For those who no longer participate in Serbian American activities, the text provides details on important holiday traditions and enough recipes to hold a feast that usually accompanies any celebration. Additionally, the chapters include cultural material that illustrates the diversity of the Serbian diaspora in Europe, which also carries over to America. Therefore, it also provides an interesting contrast for the reader to evaluate the changes that have occurred since the arrival of the immigrants. When completed, the reader should know the difference between a "kolo" and a "Sarma." From there, readers have enough information to decide if they would like to learn more about the Serbian American community.

Serbian Emigration

Beginning in the sixth century, the first Slavic groups of Serbs and Croats entered the Balkans and settled in the region between the Roman and Byzantine empires. Their choice of locations set a precedent that had far-reaching consequences for the Serbian people. Over the next thousand years, the Ottoman Turks, Croats, Austrians, Hungarians, Italians, and Bulgarians laid new claims to the same land, which in turn led to numerous battles among the rival contenders. As a community caught between rival empires, the South Slavs divided their support between the Roman Catholic West and Orthodox East that sought to dominate the region. These struggles also created a large diaspora of Serbian migrants, along with an intermingling of Roman, Byzantine, and Slavic populations in the Balkans. As a result, the Serbs emerged as a transient population with ill-defined borders, but sharing their ethnic heritage through a common language and an Orthodox religious tradition.

The process of creating a distinct Serbian homeland in the Balkans began in the twelfth century with the papal recognition of the Nemanjić dynasty under King Stephan I and the establishment of an independent Serbian Orthodox Church. The king's youngest son, Rastko, later canonized as Saint Sava, contributed to both the political and religious development of the young nation. He not only obtained recognition of an independent Serbian

Orthodox Church from the Byzantine Empire, he also wrote the nation's constitution, called the Nomocanon of St. Sava, which was based on Roman law. The close relationship between the church and government continued over the next centuries as many of the early kings were elevated to sainthood. As the Nemanjić dynasty grew in strength, the later kings, such as Stephan Dušan, expanded the territorial holdings of the Serbian Empire by taking lands away from the Byzantine and Bulgarian empires. By 1355, Dušan controlled an area from Belgrade in the north to Ragusa on the Adriatic Sea and then southward to the doorstep of Athens, including much of the Aegean coastline. This "Golden Era" of Serbian history did not last past the death of King Dušan as his son Urosch lost control over the population and the nation fell into a period of civil war that ended the Nemanjić dynasty.

Eventually Prince Lazar Hrebljanović emerged as the new leader of Serbia, and he began to form military alliances with neighboring powers, including the Bulgarians, to stop the expansion of the Muslim Ottoman Turks who had begun to replace the Byzantines as the dominant power in the Balkans. In 1389, Lazar led his army into battle against the Turks in Kosovo at the Field of Blackbirds. Lazar's untimely defeat in Kosovo brought an end to an independent Serbia as the Turks incorporated the region into their empire and established local control over the population through the creation of several sultanates in the Balkans. In the period of Turkish domination, Lazar became the martyred hero of a defeated people and the region around the city of Peć in Kosovo transformed into a religious center for the Serbian Orthodox Church to commemorate the lost battle.

In order to escape Turkish domination, several thousand Serbs moved northward to Austrian lands controlled by the Hapsburg monarchy. They established a new and independent religious center at Karlovac, in modern Croatia. The Hapsburgs fortified the region, which they referred to as the Krajina, while the local Serb, Croat, and Slovenian populations formed the first line of defense against any renewed attempts by the Turks to spread Islam into the Christian-controlled portions of Central Europe. For the Serbs, Karlovac symbolized their desire to create a new independent Serbia, while the Orthodox Church helped to foster these ideas of nationalism. The church used the religious centers in Karlovac, Peć, and Belgrade to preserve and mythologize the actions of Stephan, Saint Sava, Dušan, and Lazar. The stories of these historic figures formed the basis for Serbian identity as they endured four centuries of Ottoman domination over the once independent Serbian population.

The one exception to the Ottoman domination of the Balkans occurred in Montenegro, the highland home of the Black Mountain Serbs. The rugged terrain and fierce resistance by the population forced out the Ottomans and allowed Stefan Crnojević to set up a semi-independent state with support from the powerful Venetian city-state that bordered Montenegro to the north. The Crnojević dynasty built their political and religious capital in Cetinje and continued to rule until the early sixteenth century when they turned over control to the Orthodox bishops, who in turn created a theocratic state. The elected bishop-princes of Montenegro preserved their independence through a succession of Ottoman invasions. By the eighteenth century, Bishop-Prince Danilo Nikola Petrović made an important diplomatic move by enlisting the help of Russia's Czar Peter the Great as a political and military ally. The alliance culminated in 1799 with Russian aid leading to the official Ottoman recognition of the Montenegrin state.

With Montenegro secured, the Russians turned to the other Slavic populations in the Balkans and began to support their independence movements as well. The process was eased by the French Revolution and Napoleonic Wars, which stimulated nationalist aspirations across the continent. At the same time, living conditions in the Balkans had declined for the Serbs as the Ottoman political elite, the janissaries, cracked down on the Slavic population for protesting against a series of new taxes and obligations. In 1804, the janissaries began to arrest and execute malcontent Serbs. In response, Karađorđe Petrović, also known as "Black George" by his friends and enemies, organized an armed resistance to Ottoman rule. Karađorđe took Belgrade, executed the remaining janissaries, and then emerged as Vožd Karađorđe, the military leader of the uprising. The new Serbian leader enjoyed several early successes against the Ottomans, but when traditional Russian support declined during the heights of the Napoleonic wars, Karađorđe was forced to flee to Austria after being overrun by a large Ottoman army. He returned in 1817 to join a second uprising, but a rival leader, Miloš Obrenović, had Karađorđe killed. The event caused a dynastic struggle for control over Serbia by the Karađorđe and Obrenović families.

However, the forces that led to independence—namely, the nationalism emanating from the religious centers at Karlovac, Peć, and Belgrade,

Arise Serbia

In 1804, the poet and scholar Dositej Obradovic penned his poem "Voštani Serbije" (Arise Serbia), which became one of the patriotic verses that propelled the Serbian people to seek independence from the Ottoman Empire.

Arise Serbia
Arise, Serbia! Arise, empress!
and let your children see your face.
Make them turn their hearts and eyes on you,
and let them hear your sweet voices.

Arise, Serbia!
You fell asleep a long time ago,
And have lain in the dark.
Now wake up
And rouse the Serbs!

Raise high your imperial head,
So that land and sea may recognize you again.
Show Europe your delightful face,
As bright and cheerful as that of Venus [the morning star].

Arise, Serbia!
You fell asleep a long time ago,
And have lain in the dark.

combined with the dynastic struggles between the Karađorđe and Obrenović families, and a desire to build a modern industrial nation—led to three waves of Serbian emigration to the United States. The first wave occurred during the two decades before the start of the First World War, the second happened after a communist revolution at the close of the Second World War, and finally a third wave after the breakup of Yugoslavia.

During the years preceding the First World War, the newly independent Serbian state enjoyed a period of peace and prosperity. Once the Ottomans

Now wake up
And rouse the Serbs!

Your sister Bosnia looks upon you
And she doesn't want to offend.
Who doesn't love, he isn't afraid of God
Who gives you a lot of help

Arise, Serbia!
You fell asleep a long time ago,
And have lain in the dark.
Now wake up
And rouse the Serbs!

Herzeg's Land [Herzegovina] and Black Mount [Montenegro],
Faraway countries and sea islands
They all want heaven's help to you
All good souls are kin to you

Arise, Serbia!
You fell asleep a long time ago,
And have lain in the dark.
Now wake up
And rouse the Serbs!

left the region, the Serbs organized a merchant class and began a series of reforms that stimulated the economy. Initially, Serbian subsistence farmers worked small and isolated tracts of land that lacked transportation to markets. In order to expand food production, Miloš Obrenović welcomed the first immigrants into Serbia. By the 1860s, his son Mihailo took in migrants from Macedonia, Bosnia, and Bulgaria. Industrialization slowly followed as the Serbs opened their first factories to sew uniforms for the military, and by 1879 they began to build a railroad system to support the army, transport food, and connect the country with the rest of Europe.[1] As the economic situation gradually improved, money could be spent on other necessities such as education.

In 1800, Belgrade had only two elementary schools and no advanced Christian schools. The population, including priests, suffered from an illiteracy rate of 70 percent or more in both urban and rural areas. Education became a priority across the nation by 1885; the Serbs had compulsory elementary schools and over five thousand secondary-education students. These individuals could attend institutions that emphasized technical, law, and agricultural secondary education.[2] As the population became more literate, they began to discuss the future of the country. Ilija Garasanin emerged as one of the great ideologues and diplomats of the era. He set Serbia on a course of modernization, combining territorial expansion with the ultimate goal of uniting the ethnic centers of Belgrade, Karlovac, and Peć. By 1878, the Serbs controlled both Belgrade and Peć, which left Karlovac as the last territory needed to complete the plan. Unfortunately, Karlovac and the Krajina region remained a part of the Austro-Hungarian Empire, and to reach the territory, the Serbs would also have to control Bosnia-Herzegovina.

The Serbs in Karlovac, Krajina, and Bosnia-Herzegovina had their own problems that overshadowed ideas of unification. The Austro-Hungarians wanted to rid the area of all the South Slavs and replace them with Germanic and Hungarian populations. They increased taxes and impeded trade, with the result that the Slavic populations of the region became destitute and sought jobs in the United States to alleviate their poverty.[3] Between 1890 and 1914, the first great migration wave of thousands of Serbs, Croats, and Slovenes left the Balkans. The people who remained chafed at the injustices caused by the Austro-Hungarians and wanted either complete independence or unification with Greater Serbia.

The act set into motion events that led to the First World War and an invasion of Serbia by the Austro-Hungarian and Bulgarian armies. The combined attack defeated the Serbian army, which first evacuated to the island of Corfu off the coast of Greece, then returned to combat by fighting in Greece as an ally to England and France. In recognition of Serbian support in the war and the desire for independence of the Balkan peoples, the Treaty of Versailles led to international recognition of the Kingdom of Serbs, Croats, and Slovenes that later became Yugoslavia.

Alexander Karađorđe transitioned from being the king of Serbia to the first king of Yugoslavia. The new state finally united the ethnic and religious centers at Belgrade, Karlovac, and Peć, which made the Serbs happy but alienated the Slovene, Croat, Bosnian, and Macedonian populations. In 1934, Alexander was assassinated by a Macedonian nationalist during a visit to France. His young son Peter II then ruled with the help of the regent, Prince Paul Karađorđe. At the beginning of the Second World War, Prince Paul signed the Tripartite Pact with the fascist dictators Benito Mussolini and Adolf Hitler. The agreement allowed Axis powers to move armies through Serbia, a situation that provoked Peter II to depose the regent and take over control of the government. Hitler responded to the political change by invading Yugoslavia and Greece. German, Italian, and Bulgarian forces occupied Yugoslavia, and Peter II joined the exiled political leaders from occupied nations in England.

The Axis powers divided Yugoslavia into occupation zones and provided limited support for an independent state in Croatia and Bosnia-Herzegovina. In the remainder of Yugoslavia two factions fought for control. A royalist Chetnik group was led by General Dragoljub Mihailović, and a communist "Partizan" army was led by Josip Broz, or "Tito" among his fellow soldiers. While Mihailović sought an accommodation with the Axis armies, Tito mounted a vigorous campaign against the Germans, Italians, and Croatians. His activities led Allied commanders to switch allegiances from an inactive Mihailović to Tito and the Partizans. With Allied support, Tito freed Yugoslavia from Axis control and it emerged as the only communist nation in Europe to remain independent of the Soviet Union. After the war ended, Tito deposed King Peter II Karađorđe, convicted Mihailović of treason, and then executed him in Belgrade.

The massive casualties caused by the war, combined with the overthrow of the Karađorđe monarchy caused a second wave of emigration to the United States. Royalist Serbs and any anticommunists who disagreed with Tito joined the thousands of displaced persons who crossed Europe in search of a new home. Many chose the United States, where they could join relatives or Serbian enclaves in places such as Michigan, Minnesota, Ohio, Illinois, and California.

The people who stayed in Yugoslavia endured a period of political repression as the communist government arrested opponents, collectivized

Figure 1. King Peter II of Yugoslavia visiting Detroit in 1952. Paul Bielich, Saint Lazarus Cathedral, Detroit, Ravanica Church Archive.

agriculture, and centralized industrial growth. Tito also promoted Yugoslav nationalism as a means to end the ethnic conflicts among the nation's diverse populations. He even developed a positive relationship with the Vatican to improve relations among Catholic and Orthodox citizens. Over the next thirty years, Tito gradually loosened economic restrictions, gave greater autonomy to individual provinces, and opened up the country to international trade.

Internationally, Yugoslavia became an important doorway between the Soviet Union and the West. Since Tito's Partizans freed the country with little help from the Red Army, he had greater flexibility to conduct an independent foreign policy. After a political feud with Soviet premier Joseph Stalin, Tito began to forge closer relations with Communist China. Tito also emerged as a leader among the nonaligned states, a group of newly independent countries whose leaders did not want to choose sides in the Cold War between the United States and the Soviet Union.

After a long illness, Tito died in 1980, which set into motion the third wave of Serbian emigration to the United States. The political vacuum left in the wake of Tito's death allowed nationalism to rise among the various ethnic groups in the country. The Catholic regions of Slovenia and Croatia had the most developed industry in Yugoslavia, and the people were tired of supporting the agricultural regions in Serbia and Kosovo. Additionally, the Croats and Slovenes had greater ties with the West and a desire to join the burgeoning European Union. The Albanian population in Kosovo sought independence, along with the Bulgarian-speaking people in Macedonia. In 1987, Slobodan Milošević became leader of the Communist Party and sought to revive both nationalism and Serbian domination in Yugoslavia. His actions alienated the Slovene and Croatian populations who in 1991 declared their independence. As a nationalist, Milošević wanted to ensure that the three traditional ethnic centers in Karlovac, Peć, and Belgrade remained under Serbian control.[4]

The Balkan Wars of the 1990s developed around the cities of Karlovac in Croatia and Peć in Kosovo. The Bosnian population suffered the greatest effects of the wars as Serbian military and paramilitary forces established a corridor connecting Belgrade to Karlovac through the center of Bosnia-Herzegovina. This new "Krajina" lasted from 1990 to 1995, when Croatian military forces routed the Krajina army and forced the Serbian population to leave the region. The Dayton Peace Accords then brought peace to Bosnia-Herzegovina when Serb, Croat, and Bosnian leaders agreed to split the region into ethnic enclaves.[5] In Kosovo, fighting erupted in 1998 as the local Albanian population attempted to force the issue of independence. When the Serbian army began to push out the local population, American and European military forces intervened with a short bombing campaign that stopped the interethnic conflict. Kosovars declared their independence from Serbia in 2008, and in 2010 the International Court of Justice recognized the sovereign state of Kosovo, although the Serbian population has not followed suit.

The string of conflicts in the Balkans caused thousands of Serbs to find homes in either safer or more prosperous regions. Many chose the United States as the best place to start new communities with their friends and relatives. In Michigan, the Serbs settled in urban areas, such as Detroit, as well as in the mining regions of the Upper Peninsula. Once again, the Orthodox Church played an important role in uniting the congregants, preserving the language, and passing on their ethnic heritage to younger generations of Serbian Americans.

Serbian American Culture

The Serbian communities that developed in Michigan during the late nineteenth and early twentieth centuries were populated with individuals from the length and breadth of the Balkans. These immigrants came from diverse communities that held their own customs, dialects, and beliefs, which first shaped a new pan-Serbian population in Michigan, which in turn led to the creation of Serbian American culture. Among the Serbs who came to Michigan, the greatest cultural disparity occurred between the lowland and highland Serbian populations from the Balkans.

In Europe, two distinct groups of lowland Serbs and one group of highland Serbs developed during the period of Ottoman domination of the region. The first group proliferated around the city of Belgrade, where they absorbed some of the social, cultural, and political ideas of the occupying army. A second group left Ottoman-controlled territory and migrated north to the Austrian Empire, where the Serbian population, along with their Slovenian and Croatian neighbors, formed the Krajina region, which emerged as the first line of defense for the Viennese government. At the same time, the highland Serbs of Montenegro maintained periods of independence during the Ottoman occupation of the Balkans by fighting protracted campaigns in the Black Mountains and defeating repeated invasions. In both the lowlands and highlands, the centuries of conflict led to similarly militarized communities, but also created two distinct cultures. In the lowlands, the Serbs lived in more pastoral, organized communities governed by feudal Ottoman or Austrian officials, whereas in the mountains the Montenegrin peoples maintained premodern clan relationships, centered on specific families.

During the period of increased conflict, a majority of Serbs lived a pastoral life in rural agricultural communities, with less than 7 percent of the total population working in urban centers.[6] Some regional diversity existed among those Serbian populations in the Ottoman-controlled areas around Belgrade, compared to those in the Austro-Hungarian Krajina. The people in Belgrade adopted the local government and dress of Turkish officials, while those in the Krajina lived in a multiethnic military district that also contained large numbers of Croats and Slovenes. The ethnic, religious, and linguistic differences of the Krajina population caused an attitude of limited acceptance among the different ethnic groups that led to a relatively peaceful coexistence.[7] As a military community, the men fought together in defense of their homes, so the ethnic groups cooperated as a method of survival because the threat posed by the Ottoman Empire overshadowed any of the minor ethnic differences.

Despite these minor differences, both regions featured peasant agricultural lands dispersed around small governmental centers that also had churches and schools. The small villages then clustered around the larger market towns, which provided the peasants with a greater variety of consumer goods and entertainment. Within the villages, Serbians developed communal societies based on the *zadruga* or household, usually composed of two or more families who lived together near their fields. For example, the traditional Serbian family model of the *zadruga* consisted of an elderly couple and their adult sons, who in turn supported their own wives and children. Approximately a dozen or so people lived in these small familial groups.

The Serbs referred to the head of the family (*zadruga*) as the *starešina* who ran the household and decided on work schedules, conducted negotiations, and attended village meetings for the entire family. He controlled the buying and selling for the household, the cash, and paid the taxes. *Starešina* status belonged to the family's most intelligent father, uncle, brother, son, or nephew, and he controlled the family business until incapacitated, which in turn led to selection of a replacement. The *Starešina,* his wife, and children had the privilege of sleeping near a hearth in the central hut, while other family members lived in unheated cabins, called *vajati,* which surrounded the main building.[8]

Other buildings on the property consisted of a variety of storehouses for the wine, brandy, grain, and pork produced on the farm. In the lowland regions of the Balkans, groves of plum, pear, and apple trees provided abundant fruit for personal consumption or distillation into spirits. Peasants also had access to a variety of grapes that often ended up in great vats of wine. By the early nineteenth century, locally grown corn and wheat became the staple of peasants' diets. Moreover, the large numbers of oak trees in the region fed a plethora of pigs, which feasted on all the free acorns and therefore reduced the cost of raising pork. The poorest families had only two to four pigs, while the richest peasants owned thirty to fifty, plus twenty to fifty sheep and at least one horse.[9] In reality, though, most Serbian farmers subsisted on their crops, with little left over to sell for consumer goods found in urban centers.

In contrast to the politically organized lowland farming communities, the highland Montenegrin Serbs lived in the last clan-based society in Europe. After generations of conflict with Ottoman invaders, society divided into localized communities as village elders provided more control than a central government.[10] The harsh living conditions in the mountains were combined with the militarization of society, protracted blood feuds among the different clans, along with constant warfare against Muslims in the region. These tribal or family blood feuds could result from any type of personal insult or deprecating remark, or the much more serious accusation of seducing a woman before marriage. Blood feuds could lead to protracted conflict between the male members of the aggrieved families. Males would hunt down their enemies, kill them, then ritually decapitate the body and place the head in a nearby cemetery. The wife of the deceased had to retrieve the head to properly bury the spouse, while her family would retaliate by killing one of their opponents. These feuds lasted until both parties agreed to a settlement or one party asked for forgiveness.[11]

Relations with Muslim communities in the region only added to the chaos of the blood feuds. Montenegrin men frequently raided nearby settlements to supplement their income and pay taxes for their families. In order to provide food for their families, women often stayed at home and cultivated fields or gardens, while men stood by to watch for possible attacks by Muslims or other Montenegrins. Additionally, men were known to beat their wives to increase agricultural production or to enforce a strict moral code that permeated Montenegrin society.[12] As a result of the constant wars with Muslims, the blood feuds, and the reliance on female farm laborers, the Montenegrins failed to develop either industry or agriculture in their homelands. The weak infrastructure and lawlessness contributed to the widespread poverty in the region, along with an ability to support only a few cities other than the capital at Cetinje.

By the end of the nineteenth century, the rampant poverty in Montenegro led Prince Nikola Petrović to begin a broad modernization program for his nation. He passed laws to curb the blood feuds, raiding, and the indiscriminate killing of Muslims. Nicholas also increased educational opportunities and improved agricultural production. The modernization program resulted in a major population increase that, in turn, led to land scarcity. By 1907, overpopulation and the need to pay additional taxes for civic improvements contributed to a mass migration to America.[13]

The reasons for emigration to America by lowland Serbs differed slightly from those of their Montenegrin neighbors. Beginning in the nineteenth century, the dual issues of industrialization and nationalism contributed to the destabilization of the region. The area around Belgrade underwent rapid industrialization, which created jobs and inhibited the financial need to leave the region. However, in the Krajina, the Hungarian rulers wanted to reduce the number of South Slavs, thereby expanding the Magyar borders at the expense of the ethnic minorities in their kingdom. In order to speed up the process, Hungarian leaders made life difficult for the Krajina citizens and this led to nationalistic clashes between the two groups.[14] The end result was protracted battles over social, political, and religious differences that contributed to widespread poverty and a desire to find a better life in America. Once in the United States, Serbian immigrants began the process of rebuilding the lives they knew, while simultaneously interacting both with the Americans and with other immigrant populations. As a result, multiethnic integration ensued, causing the cultural differences between highland and lowland Serbs to recede in Michigan.

At the end of the nineteenth century, Michigan was rapidly developing into a wealthy state as robust industrial growth swelled urban centers, while

An Inn near Cetinje, Montenegro

It was a pot-house. You could not call it by a more dignified title. It had all the dirt and discomfort of a native han [cottage] and none of a han's picturesqueness. But Stana, Kristo's cousin, was inordinately proud of it. To her it represented years and years of toil to feed and educate her orphaned son, and seemed the last word in progress and civilization. It had glass windows—always shut; and an Austrian stove—always burning. It had broken-down bent wood chairs and a table with a filthy, patterned European cloth. Yet filthier European machine-lace curtains of hideous design darkened the windows. Hundreds of frowsy picture post cards and fly-blown advertisements of Italian and Austrian liquors covered the wall. Flies crawled everywhere, and rose in a frizzing mass from unwashed plates on the table when everyone moved.

Not that there was much space to move, for the room was blocked by four rickety wooden bedsteads, and untidy heaps of dull, mud-colored sheets and wadded coverlets oozing dirty rags made the close atmosphere yet more unsavory.

Except myself, no one noticed these details. The inn was reckoned one of the best in Cetinje of those which were for "the people." Stana had satisfied "a long-felt want" when she started it. Two of the four beds were let permanently to the gendarmerie at "pension" terms, so that she had a certainty to go upon; and the other two were seldom unlet. Moreover, when you have one gendarme several others are sure to call for refreshments.

Stana was busy chopping onions for a stew, which was calculated to attract the gendarmes at midday, and the smell of the onions, as they sizzled in a sea of fat, drowned the odor of stale sweat and unwashed humanity.

It penetrated even beneath the piled-up coverlets on the farther bed. They heaved, and there was a muttered oath. I had not noticed till then that the bed was occupied: "It is Mitar," said Stana. "Poor man, he was on duty till four this morning. It is really Stjepan's bed, but he is on duty now, so I have let it to Mitar for the day. One earns much this way from gendarmes. Poor lads, they have no homes here, and I have made it all nice for them."

Source: M. E. Durham, *Some Tribal Origins Laws and Customs of the Balkans* (London: George Allen and Unwin LTD, 1928), 179–80.

rural areas also benefited from logging, mining, and farming. In Detroit, Ransom E. Olds opened the first automobile factory in 1899, with Henry Ford, David Buick, the Dodge brothers, and William Durant's General Motors Company following over the next decade. The competing firms hired thousands of laborers to build nearly five million cars before the outbreak of the First World War.[15] As manufacturing increased, new factories opened in surrounding cities such as Flint, Saginaw, Lansing, and Grand Rapids. In rural Michigan, the heavily forested northern regions attracted large numbers of workers for the lumber industry, while farming regions in the south provided ample possibilities with land costing as little as five dollars an acre.[16] The Upper Peninsula also contained both copper and iron deposits near the towns in Marquette, Calumet, and Iron Mountain. During the early twentieth century, these fields produced approximately 13 million tons of copper and 18 million tons of iron ore each year.[17] This confluence of wealth and opportunity provided ample reasons to move to Michigan.

The manufacturing in Detroit and Flint, plus the mining in the Upper Peninsula attracted the largest numbers of Serbs. According to 1920 census records, approximately 2,100 foreign-born Serbs lived throughout Michigan, with approximately 1,600 in Wayne County, 85 in Genessee, and another 130 in Houghton and Gogebic Counties. When combined with a nearly equal number of naturalized Serbs, they provided a significant labor force to Michigan's economy.[18]

By the early twentieth century, a typical Serbian worker toiled long hours at mostly unskilled or semiskilled labor positions where they often faced problems of job competition, low wages, and racism from established immigrant groups and the American public. Serbs and other South Slavic workers were lumped together with other Eastern European workers by Americans, who coined the pejoratives "Bohunks" or "Hunkies," which derived from a combination of the terms Bohemian and Hungarian, to describe any South Slav.[19] The situation was made worse by the 1911 report prepared by William Dillingham for Congress that addressed the impact of immigration on the United States. The commission produced a *Statistical Review of Immigration* and a *Dictionary of Races,* both of which criticized Serbians along with all the other South Slavic populations.[20] The *Dictionary of Races* characterized Serbo-Croatians as illiterate savages with a propensity for murder and political feuds, making them ill-suited for a modern, industrial nation.[21] While the report may reflect the feelings of governmental officials and many average Americans during the period, the reality of life in Serbian ethnic enclaves proved to be much different than the low expectations expressed in Washington.

By acting on their motto, "Covek mora da radi" (A person has to work), Serbian immigrants strove to raise their economic status, which gradually improved over time.[22] A cursory examination of census records from the era illustrate that most Serbian immigrants worked as laborers. Their high rates of illiteracy and the lack of industrial working experience prevented many from obtaining more lucrative positions. As a result, early Serbian immigrants suffered from high rates of poverty. A much smaller group of Serbs obtained the education and skills to earn better jobs—such as streetcar conductor, automotive machinist, and translator—that propelled them into prominent positions in their newly adopted Michigan communities.

Within these communities, the home emerged as the focal point of daily life for Serbian immigrants. Rampant poverty forced many Serbs to live communally, in similar fashion to the *zadruga* households in the old country. The main difference, though, was the number of women who could contribute to the new communities. Among Serbian immigrants, women made up only 5 percent of the population.[23] These small numbers of Serbian women often set up boarding houses where they cared for dozens of countrymen at a time.

If an immigrant approached one of these early boarding houses, they would often find a two-story, 800-square-foot house with either clapboard or tarpaper siding. A fence usually surrounded the property, which allowed the proprietor to keep a small number of chickens or pigs nearby to feed the boarders. Yards often had gardens to supplement diets with green vegetables during the summer, while also providing a source for canned goods that could feed the family over the long winters. As the immigrants entered the dwelling, they might find three rooms on the first floor. The owners kept one room for themselves, near the kitchen, to allow women to feed the men when they returned from their shifts in the factories or mines. Some of these modest kitchens had running water and a wood-fired stove for cooking. Cooking pans and tins of food often decorated shelves and allowed the woman to quickly provide a meal to the hungry men. A makeshift dining room with peeling wallpaper, replete with mismatched chairs or bench seating, offered some of the few amenities available to lodgers. Upstairs was reserved for the many beds used by the laborers. As the boarding houses became more crowded, workers would have to rest upstairs in shifts, called "hot-cotting," where one man would sleep for eight hours, then turn over the bed to the next boarder, who could then crawl into the warm sheets. As one group of men slept, others would gather in the dining room where they could talk, eat, or play music after a long day of hard work.

These homes and boarding houses remained an important transitional tool that provided economic stability and entertainment to a generation of Serbian immigrants. Since many of the young men had little money, they could not go out for entertainment. If the boarding house provided alcohol to patrons, it was called a "saloon" or hotel. In northern mining districts, the houses that sold home-brewed spirits were called "blind pigs" in reference to people losing their vision after pickling their eyes with tainted alcohol. Nevertheless, proprietors also provided loans to people as they were one of the few groups with a steady income at the turn of the century. As a result, the boarding-house owners often emerged as early community leaders who helped to integrate Serbian workers into American society. As time progressed, these same owners expanded their services to include banking, international ticket sales (*šifikartaši*), and local politics, where their establishments provided important venues for public speaking.[24]

An example of boarding-house owners can be seen in the lives of Ilija and Sava Miljevich from Wakefield, Michigan. As was common at the time, Ilija left his home in Bosnia, arriving in Alaska during 1908, but his inability to speak English forced him to find work in a larger Serbian enclave. He then moved to Minnesota's Mesabi Iron Range and opened a saloon. After securing an income he then brought his wife and two daughters, Mara and Djuja, to Minnesota. The entire family eventually moved to Michigan, where they rented a large house and took in forty boarders to make extra money. In 1929, Ilija bought 70 acres of land and then opened a lumber mill, which provided stable employment for the entire family. When World War Two began, his sons joined the military, while his daughters first stayed home to help the family and then moved to Detroit to work in a war industry. Once the war ended, the young adults made their father proud by becoming teachers, musicians, and businessmen. The logging business flourished, and in 1960, the sons, Toto and Eli, won the First Lumberjack World Championships, held in

Hayward, Wisconsin. All of these accomplishments point to the successful integration of the entire family into American society.[25]

Not everyone believed that boarding houses served a useful purpose in American society. In Detroit, Henry Ford would play a role in changing the lives of Serbian workers. Ford developed mass-production techniques and began implementing his ideas in 1914 with the introduction of the assembly line, which allowed workers to build cars rapidly. However, workers were unhappy with repetitive work of continually attaching the same part to chassis moving down the assembly line. They also chafed at the draconian rules established by Ford that forbade talking, whistling, smoking, or sitting while working. Conditions led to such a high turnover rate that Ford increased wages to keep employees in his factories. The money not only provided workers with an opportunity to buy the cars coming off the assembly line, but attracted large numbers of immigrants to Ford's factories. Approximately 70 percent of Ford workers were immigrants, including 137 Serbs.[26] The company had its own Sociological Department, which kept track of workers' activities to prevent them from forming unions. The department also had a mission to teach immigrants how to be good middle-class Americans.

This plan was furthered by the Education Department, which taught English to workers as part of an overall plan to Americanize foreign workers. To that end, Ford wanted all of his workers to live in their own houses and not communally, as was common among South Slavs. The company condemned the practice of boarding houses because it was viewed as a backward custom, which forced the wife to constantly work and ignore her children, and ended up destroying all the joys of family life. Ford moved men and their families from ethnic enclaves into special housing around Dearborn, and then forced his employees to buy their own homes. In 1914 approximately 20 percent of Ford employees lived in boarding houses, while in 1920 only 1 percent remained in the traditional form of housing.[27]

Along with boarding houses and building cars, the mining industries in the Upper Peninsula offered a multitude of opportunities for Serbian immigrants. The copper mines surrounding Calumet, Michigan, attracted a number of young men who took a variety of jobs in the city. These included saloon owner Mile Platisa, milkman George Vranich, miner Radotovich, and trammer Marcus Gostovich, who worked in the Calumet & Hecla mines. Typically, a Serbian community builds an Orthodox church when they have enough parishioners to support the project. In Calumet, Serbs established the St. Michael Archangel Lodge #107, of the Serbian Orthodox Society, to begin the planning process. Unfortunately, the population never rose to the level where they could afford to build the church.[28] The same parishioners also worked in the region dominated by the mine owners, who owned all the land and influenced local politics.

The mine owners sought to keep production costs low, profits highs, and the laborers under control. This meant that life in mining communities could be difficult for both laborers and merchants, who could rent land and build houses or businesses, but owning land was uncommon because of the high prices in ore-rich regions. Poor working conditions in the mines led to numerous deaths and injuries. For example, in 1912 accidents accounted for 47 deaths, 643 serious wounds, and close to 4,000 slight injuries.[29] On a typical day, a Serbian worker would enter an underground mine through the shaft house and then descend on an elevator down a vertical tunnel, secured by logs. As the laborer dropped every hundred feet or so, he would see a horizontal tunnel extending outward from the central shaft. During the next ten to twelve hours, the darkened cavern would be home for work crews comprised of miners who removed the ore, and the trammers, who had to push the earth-laden carts back to the central shaft where they would wait for the elevator to take the minerals up to the surface. The earliest tunnels were only lit by candles, but as time progressed, electric lights began to illuminate the passages. Another invention that had a major impact on the development of the mining industry was the one-man drill. The new technology cut the number of workers in half, thereby putting a large number of men out of work. The unemployed and underpaid remaining workers felt helpless to confront the overwhelming power of the mine owners, leading to a rise in union activity, such as the establishment of the Western Federation of Miners in the Upper Peninsula.

In 1913, the growing animosity between mine owners and workers culminated in a protracted and bloody strike. The confrontation began in July when workers voted to walk out until their demands for union recognition, higher wages, and safer working conditions were met. James MacNaughton, superintendent of the Calumet & Hecla Mining Company, took a leading role in organizing the other mine owners in crushing the labor unrest. MacNaughton called upon the governor to send National Guard troops to police the region, while also hiring special deputies to work as strikebreakers. A series of clashes ensued that left two miners dead and a young girl grievously wounded. On Christmas Eve, a gathering of miners and their families met with a tragic end after someone shouted "Fire" at a celebration held in Calumet's Italian Hall. The resultant chaos led to seventy- three deaths as people fled the building, only to be trapped by a closed door and smothered by the panicking crowd.[30] In the end, the violence of the strikebreakers and the intransigence of the owners brought an end to the strike. The defeated workers had few choices other than to leave or go back and take the wages offered to miners.

The disillusioned miners in Michigan were just a small portion of people made unhappy by working conditions in America, leading to a radicalization of political parties and labor unions. The situation would permanently split Serbian immigrant communities into two factions. On one side of the divide stood churchgoing, politically conservative Serbs, who readily conformed to American societal norms. They went to work, often joined fraternal organizations and labor unions, and also participated in cultural assimilation groups such as the Yugoslav Education Society, Montenegrin Educational Club, or Yugoslav American Independent Club. The fraternal unions played an important role in mitigating some of the harsh living and working conditions found in industrial cities. By pooling their finances, Serbs could obtain resources they could not afford individually, such as insurance for health care or to cover the cost of burials. Early examples were the Serbian-Montenegrin Literary and Benevolent Society in San Francisco, the First Serbian Brotherhood Benevolent Federation of America, and the Serbian National Federation (Srpski Narodni Savez).

These large benevolent societies often comprised numerous local organizations. The Serbian National Federation (SNF) began in the late nineteenth century as an autonomous group, but grew in size by incorporating several independent organizations under the leadership of Simo Vrlinich, Louis Christopher, and Mile Radakovich. By 1929 the SNF had approximately twenty thousand members throughout the nation. They maintained the same level of participation into the 1970s by attracting younger generations of Serbian immigrants. They accomplished the feat by offering language classes and sporting events, such as golf, bowling, and basketball.[31] In this manner, the SNF helped to transition Serbian immigrants into American

Underground in America

I pray that God may grant me sufficient skill in writing to express to my people in the old country what we know here in America.

Many people in my native land desire to immigrate to America. Which they depict in their imagination as a land of great opportunity and a heaven on earth, just as I did before my arrival here.

My idea in coming to America was to go underground, into the mines to dig gold, and after spending some time in this labor, to return to the land of my fathers.

But I see now what a terrible mistake I made by not staying in the old country.

Life and work are very hard underground without light and air. But still it would not be right to speak against this rich, beautiful and free country, which gives equal rights to poor and rich, strong and weak.

But for us Serbians this land is cold, and our life here is miserable for many reasons.

We immigrants must forget all that we have learned, and we must so to speak be born again and transport ourselves to another world.

Because we do not know English, we must work hard to learn it; for English is harder than stone. No language in the whole world is more difficult. Americans speak like toothless old women, like cows chewing hay. Both ears must be kept wide open if you want to understand anything. Your mouth must be twisted, and

citizens while maintaining their cultural heritage among second-, third-, and fourth-generation Serbian Americans.

Serbian immigrants who supported syndicalism, socialism, and communism attempted a more radical solution to the difficulties found in American life. Instead of adopting American social norms, they demanded a complete transformation of the nation's political and economic systems. The syndicalists formed the Industrial Workers of the World (IWW) in 1905, under the leadership of William "Big Bill" Haywood. He was a firm believer in a unified workers' organization, as expressed in their slogan, "One Big Union." In order to achieve their goals of better wages and working conditions, the IWW used a tactic called direct action, whereby they would go out on strike and cause *your tongue squeezed in order to pronounce English words properly. If one is looking for a job and does not have a friend to help him, he may spend 3 whole years and travel a thousand miles without finding work, and God save him from utter destitution! When you are without work in America, you realize what a mistake you made in leaving home. Suppose you get a job in a mine. Then you shall see how your health will be ruined, for mines are worse than prisons, and air has to be pumped into them by machinery. Rocks menace you with death, there is none of the sunshine that you love. Candles are forever burning; your eyes are blinded with smoke; poisonous gas fills your lungs. But even this is not the worst, for in summer the mines are filled with water.*

After working in a mine, you will be glad to be a shepherd, eating only one meal a day but breathing the clear, pure air above ground.

In mines there is eternal night and darkness quickly kills your youth, depletes your energy, endangers your life, and destroys your ambition. We look like dead men, pale and weak.

After so bitter an experience I no longer desire to gain gold but only to do something full of life and enjoyment. Let my work be in the sunshine, where there is plenty of pure air, even though the wages be small!

May this account of my experience help you be wise!

Source: Lazar Church, "Underground in America," pamphlet, 1907, available at http://www.freewebs.com/cikaskisrbi/en/chicago_serbs_timeline.pdf.

discord until their demands had been met by management. The organization offered immigrants denied voting rights by their lack of citizenship a way to improve their lives outside the bounds of the American political system. This made the IWW very popular among first-generation immigrants, especially those in the mining, iron, and manufacturing industries.

In 1914, the IWW began a drive to organize auto workers in Detroit over the strenuous objections of Henry Ford and the other manufacturers in the city. Organizers found little support at the Ford plants, so they moved on to Studebaker workers in nearby factories. While both the Ford and Studebaker employees were unhappy with their wages and working conditions, approximately two hundred Studebaker workers joined the IWW's Local 16 and began to distribute literature to attract more men to the organization. In June, the workers demanded weekly wages and an eight-hour workday. When Studebaker's management rejected the demand, approximately six thousand men staged a short week-long strike. While they did not achieve the demands that led to the strike, Studebaker provided workers with some of their wages on a weekly basis, while Ford initiated a five-dollar-a-day wage to prevent any renewed union activity in his plants.[32]

Serbian immigrants played a much larger and more active role in the socialist and communist movements. Eugene Debs, who helped found the IWW, also established the American Socialist Party (ASP) and actively recruited foreign socialist movements into his umbrella organization. In the case of Serbian workers, in 1909 they established the South Slavic Socialist Federation of America at a meeting held in Pittsburgh, Pennsylvania. By 1913 they had joined the larger ASP and reported to the national headquarters that the South Slavs had approximately 1,800 members, including 164 Serbs.[33] Overall membership increased to 4,000 members by 1917, with locals in Calumet and Detroit.[34] However, internal dissent and governmental repression led to the factionalization of the federation after the First World War. Some individuals in 1929 created Detroit's Yugoslav Industrial Alliance, while others formed a Serbian chapter of the American Communist Party. Individuals such as Joso Rajnovich, Mirko Markovich, and Srdja Prica organized the first communist local in Milwaukee, where they also published their newspaper *Slobodna Rec* (Free Expression).[35] All of these activities were viewed as disloyal by most Serbs, and especially by the American government.

During the First World War, the American government cracked down on radical groups for their antiwar stance, and after 1917 to thwart a possible communist revolution in the United States. Both Eugene Debs and William Haywood were arrested and jailed during the war for their anti-government activities. Haywood eventually fled to the Soviet Union, where he joined communist leader Vladimir Lenin and his Russian Bolshevik Revolution. Americans feared that the Bolsheviks' communist ideas would be transmitted to the United States among Slavic and Eastern European immigrants. Therefore, Congress began to enact legislation to curtail new immigration. The 1917 Immigration Act placed much stricter rules on who could become an American. The law barred anarchists, criminals, the mentally handicapped, and illiterates from entering the United States. On September 16,

Figure 2. Detroit's Serbian population pledged $35,000 in war bonds during a WJBK radio program. Overall, the community purchased $159,000 in bonds. Working on the bond sales committee were, left to right: Dr. Stanley Papich; Mrs. Ella Sargin; Mrs. Ann Papich; and the Rev. Firmilian Ocokoljich, pastor of the Detroit Serbian Orthodox Church. Paul Belich, Saint Lazarus Cathedral, Detroit, Ravanica Church Archive.

1920, suspected leftists exploded a bomb on Wall Street in New York City, killing thirty-eight people and injuring hundreds more. This and similar incidents soured public opinion toward all immigrants, including Serbs. Congress responded to the incidents with the 1921 and 1924 Johnson-Reed Acts, which placed limits on the number of South Slavic and Eastern European immigrants allowed into the United States because of their suspect loyalty and low literacy rates.[36] These "Red Scare" laws and a widespread fear of communism also led to the mass arrests of approximately ten thousand suspected immigrant subversives and the deportation of over two hundred radicals, who ended up in Russia with William Haywood.[37] Despite the negative public opinion concerning immigrants in general, Serbian communities throughout Michigan continued to assimilate into American culture.

By the 1930s, Michigan's Serbian population continued to grow, reaching approximately 44,000 first- and second-generation immigrants in the state.[38]

In 1940, Detroit alone had 3,360 Serbs clustered in the Clairpointe, Cottage Grove, and Fenkell, McNichols, and Russell neighborhoods.[39] The number of Serbian Orthodox churches increased, along with the schools, halls, civic groups, and social institutions that helped transmit Serbian heritage to children born in America. Changes also occurred at a rapid pace. Interfaith marriage became more common because of the limited number of Serbian women. The English language came to dominate in Serbian communities as children sought to be more like their American neighbors.

When war in Europe broke out again in 1939, Serbians again showed their American patriotism. Approximately 50,000 South Slavs joined the military during the Second World War, while others worked in factories, building the ships, airplanes, and tanks needed to destroy the German, Italian, and Japanese armies that threatened the country.[40] With victory achieved in 1945, most Americans returned to their homes and resumed the lives they knew before the upheavals caused by war. For Serbian Americans, their community would be transformed by large numbers of Yugoslavian refugees, who would embroil the population in a religious and political battle over the legitimacy of the Serbian Orthodox Church.

Following the Second World War, Europe was convulsed with thousands of refugees displaced by the fighting and fleeing oppression, or they were ethnically cleansed from regions occupied by the Soviet army and then moved to Germany. Among them, approximately 443,000 people fled Marshal Tito's communist takeover of Yugoslavia.[41] In order to address the European crisis, the United States Congress passed a series of laws, including the 1948 Displaced Persons Act, the 1953 and 1960 Refugee-Escapee Acts, and the 1965 Refugee Conditional Entrants Act, that regulated the influx of new immigrants coming to America. The Displaced Persons Act required immigrants to find a sponsor—either a possible employer, public or private agency, relative, or friend. Sponsors had to prove that immigrants had a job, housing, transportation, and give assurances that the individual would not become indigent, requiring government assistance. A further obstacle to immigration was that all of these steps had to be accomplished without displacing an American worker. Initially, people had to obtain permission for individual refugees, but when this proved unwieldy, groups received blanket assurances.[42]

The Serbian Orthodox Diocese and the Serbian National Defense League took an active role in bringing refugees to America. The organizations received an interest-free loan of $200,000 from the federal government to help relocate Serbs in the United States.[43] The latest wave of immigrants differed from those who arrived at the turn of the twentieth century in several key areas. Whereas women made up only a small percentage of early immigrants, the postwar influx had nearly equal numbers of males and females. Education levels had also increased, and most Serbs arrived in America literate and often trained by military service, although individuals still had to learn English. The program was considered a success because of the high number of professionals among the immigrants, and the vibrant American postwar economy that allowed people to find good, high-wage jobs in urban areas.[44]

Between 1946 and 1968, approximately 66,000 Yugoslavs immigrated to the United States.[45] In Michigan, Serbs moved to established immigrant neighborhoods in Detroit, Clairpointe, Cottage Grove, Fenkell, McNichols, and Russell. However, the recent arrivals and second-generation Serbian Americans did not agree on all aspects of community development. Some differences were easy to accommodate. Recent arrivals enjoyed soccer and accordion music, while Serbian Americans preferred basketball and *tamburitza* bands. Other issues, especially concerning religion, took much longer to overcome. The Serbian American population began to question some of the traditions in the Serbian Orthodox Church. Debates began over the inclusion of American music alongside traditional Serbian hymns, whether priests should keep their beards or shave, and if Sunday schools should teach both religion and nationalism to children. The new Serbian immigrants rejected the changes, while also criticizing the American-born population for not supporting Serbia in overthrowing the communist government. These differences caused greater alienation between the two groups, leading to increased conflict, which caused many third-generation immigrants to leave the church rather than continually fight with their neighbors.[46]

The issue of communism further divided the Serbian American community of Detroit during the early phase of the Cold War. After the Second World War victory celebrations had ended, Michigan's Serbian population entered into a golden age of economic growth and prosperity. Factories turned out new cars and consumer goods to feed the desires of returning veterans and their growing families. American industry also helped to rebuild the infrastructure destroyed by war in Europe and Asia. During this bountiful time, a growing fear of communism, fostered by the beginning of the nuclear arms race between the United States and the Soviet Union, the division of Europe into two armed camps, and a series of wars in Asia, led to a dark chapter in American history. Wisconsin senator Joseph McCarthy used the crises to further his flagging political career by raising the specter of an imminent threat of a communist takeover of the United States, leading to a period known as the Red Scare. Between 1950 and 1954, McCarthy parlayed unsubstantiated claims of communist infiltration of the American government into seats on the Tydings Commission and the Permanent Subcommittee on Investigations (PSI), where he conducted public hearings on suspected communists. At the same time, the House Un-American Activities Commission (HUAC) held similar trials that also featured public denunciations of suspected communists, demands for the names of accomplices, and lack of judicial protections for the accused. These conditions led to an era of fear, accompanied by new laws that impinged on civil rights in order to create the feeling of greater public safety.

At the federal level, the 1940 Smith Act was initially aimed at stopping German and Italian fascist groups from advocating the overthrow of the American government during the Second World War. However, with the onset of the Cold War in 1947 and the increased fear of communism, the Smith Act became one of the favored tools for convicting suspected communists of subversion and sending them to jail. In Michigan, the state legislature passed the "Little Smith Act" in 1952, which made advocating the overthrow of the American government punishable by life in prison. The Trucks Act required all communists to register with the government; failure to do so could lead to extensive jail time. Additionally, the American Bar Association made great efforts to disbar lawyers suspected of communist sympathies. The end result was a period when lawyers could not afford to defend persons accused of disloyalty for fear of losing their own jobs, while anyone could be publicly excoriated by allegations of communist sympathies.[47]

In 1953, Air Force Lieutenant Milo Radulovich, a member of Michigan's Serbian community, played a major role in the political downfall of Joseph McCarthy and the Red Scare. Milo's father, Jovan (John) Radulovich, a Montenegrin immigrant, was anonymously accused of disloyalty for reading the leftist newspaper *Slobodna Rec* (Free Expression) and advocating communism at his job working on the assembly line at the Hudson Motor

Car Company. Furthermore, Margaret, Milo's sister, had participated in civil rights protests, opposed the Smith Act, and belonged to a series of progressive movements.[48] Because of accusations leveled at his family, Lt. Radulovich was considered a security threat by the United States Air Force and asked to resign from the military. Instead of leaving in shame, Lt. Radulovich decided to fight for his name and family honor.

Milo attempted to retain a lawyer, but most members of Michigan's legal community refused to accept the case. Eventually, Charles Lockwood and Ken Sanborn agreed to represent Lt. Radulovich at his military hearing to decide whether the officer could keep his commission. The poisoned atmosphere surrounding any accusation of communist support forced Lockwood to address public opinion if there were to be any chance of success. Lockwood contacted the *Detroit News* and shared Milo's story with the editors. They in turn wrote sympathetic stories of a young American veteran, with a wife and children, struggling to support his family while attending classes at the University of Michigan. They discussed Jovan's limited language skills, pointing out that he read both liberal and conservative Serbian newspapers to follow events in Yugoslavia. As a loyal American, Jovan voted for President Franklin Roosevelt, joined a union, and supported his fellow workers, even accepting a temporary layoff to allow a wounded veteran to retain his job.[49]

When the military hearing began, Lockwood and Sanborn challenged the legality of the procedures, as a way to set up a legal appeal after what they felt was the impending defeat of their case. Nevertheless, the lawyers put up a spirited defense, which allowed Milo, Jovan, and Margaret to address questions from military officials. Jovan even received help from the Hudson Car Company, which sent representatives who spoke of his good character. As the hearing gained notoriety and public support in the *Detroit Free Press* and *Detroit Times*, *Time* magazine picked up the story, helping to transform a local problem into a national issue.[50]

Edward R. Murrow, one of the best-known reporters of the era, also featured the Radulovich saga on his television program, *See It Now*. The combined bad press led Americans to reconsider their support for Joseph McCarthy and challenge the way he treated suspected communists. While Radulovich lost the official hearing in October 1953, the Air Force reinstated his commission a month later, when a firestorm of public support following Murrow's television program led to widespread complaints about the military's conduct in the affair. Murrow then went on to feature another program on McCarthy, which effectively criticized the senator's conduct, leading to a fall in his popularity. In 1964, McCarthy came under attack from both the United States Army and fellow senators who officially censured him for his conduct during the search for communists. While McCarthy retained his position in the Senate, he lost the respect of his peers and Wisconsin voters. He returned home in 1956, only to die in ignominy the following year.

The Milo Radulovich story illustrated not only the bravery of one man against an unjust political and legal system, but also the extent of Americanization among Michigan's Serbian immigrant population. By standing up for his family and name, Radulovich demonstrated the warrior customs of his Montenegrin ancestors. This can be seen again when he was confronted with intimidation by military officials who demanded that he resign his commission as an Air Force officer due to unproven allegations. However, instead of resorting to violence as was customary in Montenegro, Radulovich made use of his constitutional rights as an American citizen. This was done completely through established legal means. He did not try to re-create the United States into a communist or socialist state as individuals in Serbian American communities had attempted to do earlier in the century. Clearly, the Radulovich family had Americanized. They spoke English, protected the nation, followed the laws, worked hard, and raised their families—all traits admired by Americans. The family, like so many others in the Serbian community, had embraced American culture as loyal citizens. However, they had not completely discarded their Serbian heritage. Serbs retained their language, religion, and some of their customs. In all, by the 1950s, first- and second-generation immigrants viewed themselves as Americans or Serbian Americans. The trend would continue into the third, fourth, and fifth generations.

Serbian Women

The contributions of Serbian women to community development have been in many ways overshadowed by those of men. Notwithstanding their small numbers relative to men, women played a major role in improving the lives of Serbian immigrants in Michigan. The position of women in the community first reflected social ideas learned in their diverse hometowns. Some of the greatest differences can be seen in the customs of lowland and highland Serbs, similar to the case of men from the same regions. However, Serbian women did share a trait with women throughout Europe and America, as they coordinated all work within the house to the point that villagers used to say, "In the house the woman is the head and the man is the guest."[51] The church represented one of the few socially acceptable venues for women to work outside the home. Once these women arrived in Michigan, they too began a transformation from their traditional roles. Women continued to work in both the home and in church, but demanded more social responsibilities and a greater voice in community development.

Over a century ago, in traditional Serbian homes, the desire to have children and expand families gave women some power. However, the societal emphasis on having boys relegated women to an inferior yet still important position. This began at birth, with clear favoritism paid to male children who would work and carry on the family name. If a father had only girls, he was seen as a very unfortunate individual. Nevertheless, all children were well cared for by their extended family. Infants usually spent their first year swaddled in cloth to ensure straight legs. Because the parents were usually working in the fields, grandparents took care of the young children. Once a child could walk and talk, they were given a lot more freedom to move around the house and fenced-in yard. Around age five, they began working around the farm tending animals, picking fruits and vegetables, and gathering firewood. At seven years old, school began, with students attending their first eight grades locally and then moving on to upper classes. As they neared adolescence, teens took on more responsibilities that also split tasks along gender lines. Boys began working more in the fields, learning how to plow, hoe, reap, and plant, plus gaining business experience by bringing goods to market. Girls took on more domestic tasks as they learned how to cook, bake, sew, and knit in preparation for married life.[52]

The average age for marriage among Serbian girls was nineteen, while boys usually waited until they were twenty-five before taking a wife. If a woman remained unmarried at thirty, neighbors considered her an "old maid." In order to prevent that from happening, parents started looking for possible spouses when she was around seventeen, when they bought the best possible clothes affordable and then began attending fairs or other suitable social gatherings to find a suitable mate.[53] Before the First World War, marriages were arranged by the two family heads, but that practice ended during the interwar era. In preparation for the impending nuptials, women filled a painted hope chest with clothes for their new married life. Later, the types of items brought to the marriage expanded to include household items such as beds, chairs, and tables.

The groom's family also prepared for the wedding ceremony by cooking a pig, while gathering materials for the reception party by borrowing tables, linens, chairs, and benches from the neighbors. Meanwhile, the groom's father had the pleasant task of bottling his best brandy. The father then embarked on a traveling tour of all the important guests, including the godfather (*kum*), witnesses, and other people associated with the wedding. At each stop the father and guests imbibed the brandy, turning the event into a festive occasion. On the wedding day, guests gathered the bride and brought her to the ceremony, carried in a caravan of flower-covered horses and buggies. During the trip, a wedding jester sang songs, joked, and made noises to promote cheer and merriment on the way to the church. The actual wedding ceremony took only a short time; afterward the wedding party and guests returned to the groom's home for the celebration. In a final symbolic gesture to her new life and family, the bride had to first hold a baby, then throw handfuls of corn in the four cardinal directions. She also threw corn on the roof of the house as a form of blessing her new home. She then picked up two loaves of bread and two bottles of wine and brought them into the house.[54]

After the ceremony and reception, the new bride had to be initiated into the new family. She demonstrated her respect by nightly washing the feet of the male elders and serving dinners. She was not entrusted with cooking and could not eat with the family, being relegated to the kitchen until everyone had finished their meal. Afterwards, the new bride would eat the leftovers alone. These customs continued in other aspects of family life. She arose earlier than the other family members and worked diligently all day long. Only after everyone had retired for the night was she allowed to go to bed. While married, the newlyweds were not considered man and wife until she had her first baby. With the arrival of a child, age, and experience, the bride slowly gained respect and stature in the family. Outwardly, this manifested itself in the woman dressing in darker colors as she aged over time.[55]

In the Montenegrin highlands, women also played an important yet subservient role in the family. They cooked and cleaned in the home, while also working in the fields to grow the crops to feed the family. A major difference between lowland and highland culture was the emphasis on maintaining family honor and heroism (*Cojstvo i junaštvo*), which were the building blocks of society.[56] For men, that meant fighting in blood feuds and seducing women from neighboring clans. However, a seduced woman was viewed as having dishonored her family, which would lead male family members to hunt down and kill the seducer. In effect, the cultural contradiction of trying to protect the chastity of female family members while actively pursuing other women caused many of the social problems in nineteenth-century Montenegro.

Women were not solely the object of dishonor; they too could actively protect the family's honor. In a blood feud, men did most of the fighting. If a married man died in battle, his wife could seek revenge by killing the person responsible for the death of her spouse. In Montenegrin culture, women in the family did not have to slay their enemies, but it was not discouraged. Women had an advantage in fighting because it was considered dishonorable to kill them—thus they could attack a man without fear of reprisal. This created a system where women often supported their husbands' feuding activities. It became common for wives to carry the straw used to burn down their enemy's house. Furthermore, any woman who participated in the actual killing of an adversary in blood revenge (*krvna osveta*) was viewed as a heroine. If her son or husband were killed, she would have surviving members of the family seek revenge. If her children were too small, she would keep a bloody article of clothing to show her son, until he grew old enough to carry a gun and exact vengeance.[57]

In order to participate in such activities, training began at an early age. Children learned that any display of emotion by women or men was a sign of weakness. Both genders had to be strong and brave to protect their honor. One way to instill outward composure in a crisis was to bathe girls in cold water. By remaining calm in an uncomfortable situation, women learned to be docile and self-controlled. This would later help them remain cool when dealing with men and preserving their own honor. While men had complete sexual freedom, any woman foolish enough to be seduced could be killed by her family if it resulted in pregnancy. A woman was expected to remain a virgin until marriage. In her new role, a young wife followed her husband's orders without complaint, while men did not take any instructions from women.[58]

The issue of honor also played a major role in determining who could marry. When Montenegrin families made marriage arrangements, they practiced a form of social eugenics. The groom's family would search for a woman from a good family, going so far as to research their history and activities over the previous century. If the girl came from several generations of brave men and beautiful women, then she would be a suitable choice, as Montenegrins believed that "marry nobodies and you'll have nobodies around your hearth."[59] Once the research had concluded, the heads of household would meet and arrange the wedding. While the bride could legally refuse the prospective groom, this usually did not happen, because the girl would not oppose the will of her family.

The two families worked together to ease the jarring transition from daughter to young bride at an unfamiliar family home through a protracted ritual. The groom's male family members collected the maiden and her brother, who had the duty of giving his sister to her new husband during the marriage ceremony. Traditionally, the bride's family did not attend the ceremony, nor did any females from the groom's side of the family. The ceremony itself lasted only a few minutes and then the bride and groom retired to the reception party. It was customary at the time for the husband to refrain from consummating the marriage for several days or longer. This helped the woman acclimate to her environment, while also proving the honor of the groom's family. If any male in the family were to make the slightest overture to the bride it would dishonor the bride's family and lead to the death of the transgressor. The wife would eventually be given permission to sleep with her husband by her new family. Afterwards, she had to provide a male heir to cement her position in the family.

When Serbian women immigrated to Michigan, they continued these traditional roles as homemakers and innkeepers. In addition, others took positions as domestics or even in factories. In 1900, approximately 72,600 women worked in Detroit, of which only 3 percent were married.[60] Women generally worked day jobs to help provide added income to support their families, especially among the working poor. At the time, an unmarried girl usually gave her father whatever wages she earned over the course of a month.

In Detroit, approximately 25 percent of women worked as tobacco strippers, basically pulling leaves from plant stalks, which was the lowest-paying job in the city; workers made only $117 each year at the San Telmo, Wayne Cigar, and Lilies Cigars factories.[61] Slavic women, especially immigrants from Poland, dominated positions at these cigar factories. Managers frequently hired women from other Slavic groups to feed the growing demand for cigars among smokers in Chicago. These women were often the single daughters of factory workers, normally under the age of twenty because they left after marriage. As competition for workers increased through the early twentieth century, owners began to build new, clean factories to attract and keep workers. The workers enjoyed a number of amenities, unheard of among older immigrants. They had showers, steel lockers, lunch rooms, drinking fountains, and occasionally readers or musicians. As wages increased by raises and promotions, women could expect to make ten dollars a week.[62]

Figure 3. Mrs. Radojhka Petroleus hands out certificates of merit signed by the Queen Mother to thirty-five Serbian women for their role in relief operations for Yugoslavian war refugees. Paul Bielich, Saint Lazarus Cathedral, Detroit, Ravanica Church Archive.

In the 1930s, second-generation immigrant women were beginning to express their own ideas and reject some of the ideas of their parents. One area of conflict was the Americanization of courtship rituals and marriage. While families actively sought out Serbian husbands for their daughters using traditional methods, the girls quickly realized that American men treated their wives with greater respect and equality than many Serbian men. Having the legal freedom to make their own choice in spouses, daughters took into account the quality of Serbian men, their income, and their general attitude toward women. They wanted decent men, capable of feeding their families without government assistance. This attitude caused a great deal of consternation among first-generation immigrants who had difficulty accepting marriage outside of the Orthodox faith or Serbian heritage. A common attitude among traditionalists was, "Why can't she get a Serb?" The answer was that women would like to share the same language, but it was no longer a requirement. Instead, Serbian women began to question whether they should follow parents' advice or use their best judgment when picking a spouse.[63] Ultimately, many women chose their own opinion over tradition in Serbian communities.

Outside of home and work, church was one of the socially acceptable places for unaccompanied women to visit at the turn of the century. Closely related to church attendance were the numerous civic and social-reform organizations created by Serbian women. Oftentimes, these organizations operated in conjunction with local churches and priests. One of the most prominent of these groups was the Circle of Serbian Sisters (Saveza Kola Srpskih Sestara), which was founded on the model of Serbian heroines such as Mother Yugovich (Majka Jugovic), who lost nine sons in the Battle of Kosovo, and the Maiden of Kosovo (Kosovoka Devojka), a nurse from the same battle who emerged as an example of Christian samaritan love.[64] The organization was initially founded in 1903, at a meeting held in Belgrade. Two women, an artist named Nadezda Petrovich and Delfa Ivanich, the wife of a foreign ministry official, wanted to provide relief for Serbian minority groups in the Ottoman and Austro-Hungarian Empires. From humble beginnings, the number of circles increased to 160 during the interwar years.[65] The Serbian Sisters first gained notoriety from publishing calendars with nationalistic themes to fund relief operations. During the First World War, members expanded their activities to include nursing wounded soldiers, operating an invalid hospital, and constructing a boarding house for young girls who had lost their fathers during the fighting. In the postwar era, Queen Marija Karađorđević, mother of King Peter II of Yugoslavia, became the honorary life president of the Circles of Serbian Sisters. Her leadership, especially during the Second World War, made her popular among Serbian populations in Europe and America.

In the United States, the first Circle of Serbian Sisters emerged in 1907 among immigrant women in Pittsburg, Pennsylvania. By 1945, the number expanded to thirty, with chapters in every major Serbian enclave in America, including Milwaukee, Duluth, and Detroit.[66] In 1945, Mrs. Nada Rashovich united the various chapters in a national movement called the American Federation of Serbian Sisters Circles of St. Sava Monastery. The women established their national headquarters in Libertyville, Illinois, which was also the religious capital of the Serbian Orthodox Church in North America. Rashovich was elected the organization's first president and remained in

Figure 4. American-born children are learning to speak Serbian at Detroit Serbian School in Clairpointe. These classes helped to create bilingual families and preserve the Serbian language. Paul Bielich, Saint Lazarus Cathedral, Detroit, Ravanica Church Archive.

office until 1949, when Ljuba Bjelajac took control. Their leadership helped to coordinate activities at the local level, making the circles a more effective organization.

The women who participated in the various local affiliates soon became the backbone of their enclaves by supporting their churches and communities. At Detroit's Ravanica Church, Pela Vranjanin called together thirty women in October 1934 to create a circle (*kolo*) for their neighborhood parish. They named the organization Serbian Sisters Ravanica (Sestre Srpkinje Ravanice), which also worked with the nearby Clairpointe neighborhood's Circle of Queen Mary (Kolo Kraljica Marija) and the Russell Street Serbian Association (Udruzenje Srpkinje). These women coordinated relief efforts for those who had been made destitute by the Great Depression. They also sought to practice their faith and preserve Serbian customs and language while passing their ethnic heritage on to the next generation.[67] This can be seen in the work of Sophie Hornovich and later of Helen Lukov, who set up the first Sunday School in the 1940s and founded the Ravanica Mothers' Club to raise funds and send children to summer camp. They also encouraged children to attend church, staged special performances, sponsored charity bazaars, and helped with funerals and weddings.[68]

During the Second World War, the Sisters joined forces with the Red Cross to support American soldiers deployed overseas to fight fascism in Europe and Asia. Using borrowed sewing machines and their own knitting needles, the women spent four years making clothing for the troops. They also raised money and purchased over $159,000 in bonds to help with the war effort. Their yeoman service in providing clothing and other necessities for Serbian war refugees resulted in a personal visit by the Queen Mother, honorary president of the Circles of Serbian Sisters, who awarded Red Cross certificates of merit to thirty-five women from Detroit. After the war, they continued to help displaced persons throughout Europe.[69]

Along with supporting soldiers, the women of Detroit helped to pay for the remodeling of St. Sava Monastery, which was also home to a Serbian heritage camp that the Circles of Serbian Sisters helped to build in order to pass on their heritage to the next generation of children. In 1942, Bishop Dionisije blessed the new facility, while Jeromonah Nikolaj Dazgich, a local parish priest, taught Serbian language, catechism, and singing classes. By 1945, attendance had grown to fifty-six boys and fifty-seven girls, while the curriculum had changed to emphasize Orthodox Christian leadership among Serbian American children. The hope was to create the next generation of civic leaders in Serbian American communities throughout the United States.[70]

As more communities sent their children to Libertyville, the accommodations needed to be enlarged. Federation president Ljuba Bjelajac began a donation drive in 1949, holding auctions for a car, television, and vacuum cleaner to raise funds. Still short of money to finish the project, the Serbian Brothers Help (Srpska Bratska Pomoc) volunteered their services in completing the interior spaces. By 1953, with construction done, the expanded facilities offered older teenagers an opportunity to learn about their heritage and faith. A high point in the history of the camp occurred in 1959, when King Peter II visited Libertyville. The king and his son, Crown Prince Alexander, spent a week at the camp, thoroughly enjoying the experience.

Unfortunately, the peaceful relations of the 1950s turned to animosity in the 1960s as the Serbian Sisters Circles split over loyalty to Bishop Dionisije or Patriarch German. Andja Polich, elected president of the federation in 1960, initially attempted to incorporate all the North American circles into the national organization. However, the growing animosity between Dionisije and German spilled over into the circles. In 1963, when the Serbian Orthodox community split, the Federation of Serbian Sisters Circles divided into two opposing factions, with Andja Polich aligning with Dionisije. The women of Ravanica helped to establish the Federation of the Circle of Serbian Sisters for the Midwest Diocese and supported the women of the Eastern American and Canadian Diocese.[71]

By 1965, approximately fifty-five circles with 2,700 members sided with Polich, who earned the nickname "Kuma," or godmother, for her work in the organization.[72] The name "Kuma" was a great honor for Polich. It referred to the tradition of godparenthood (*Kumstvo*) and the selection of a godfather (*Kum*) and godmother (*Kuma*) who had the responsibility for the spiritual upbringing of the child and would assume a parental role if the mother and father died or were incapacitated by injury.[73] The title was also awarded to important leaders in organizations, and was an accolade Polich received for generosity to Serbian Americans and the Circle of Serbian Sisters. She gave over $1 million to the church, helped to build over a dozen churches and halls, founded the newspaper *Diocesan Observer,* and raised money for legal cases.[74] In 1968, Polich gave the Serbian Sisters an $80,000 house in Jackson, California, for the women to dedicate themselves completely to the St. Sava Mission role of serving children.[75] In February 1970 she died of heart failure and was buried at the Jackson mission with 1,500 people attending, including two bishops.[76] Mary Stepanovich replaced her as the president of the Free Diocese's Circle of Serbian Sisters. Regardless of leadership, the women continued their charitable work for the Serbian American community.

Despite the conflict within the Serbian Orthodox Church, the women in Michigan continued their work as well. In the 1960s and 1970s, the construction and furnishing of the new Saint Lazarus Cathedral in Detroit required a great deal of attention. The United Serbian Women (Udruzene Srpkinje) purchased two bells for the cathedral, whereas the Serbian Sisters provided the stained glass, a mosaic of Mary, portraits of the Twelve Apostles, a tabernacle, icon stands, and the Holy Water Font.[77] In a 1971 ceremony, Ravanica's Detroit Women's Club president Pat Drekich and Stella Raicevich held a ceremony to burn the $22,000 mortgage papers for the church pews that they had just paid in full.[78] In addition to furbishing the Ravanica church, the women also made time to raise funds to support other organizations, including churches, circles, lodges, and camps. Their generosity and support of community development remain hallmarks of their current mission.

Regardless of the political and religious disputes that rocked Serbian enclaves, the women continued their work nurturing the disaffected and improving lives. For over a century in Europe and America, the Circle of Serbian Sisters, along with the United Serbian Women and other groups, served as guardians of Serbian culture and heritage. At the same time, they also took on more American characteristics by becoming more self-assertive, which can be seen in their choice of marriage partners, and by assuming leadership roles in their communities. Over the course of the twentieth century, Serbian women made great strides toward greater equality. In the nineteenth century, a Serbian bride toiled long hours cooking and cleaning for her husband's extended family. However, second- and third-generation Serbian American women rejected many of their traditional roles in the home by moving outward to include community development. This created generations of women who celebrate the past while embracing modern society.

Religious Celebrations and Conflicts

Within Serbian society, the Orthodox faith has played a central role in ethnic identity for hundreds of years. In the Balkans, Orthodoxy differentiated Serbs from their Bosnian Muslim, Slovenian, and Croatian Catholic neighbors. When Serbian immigrants arrived in Michigan, the tradition continued as they built new churches, which formed the hearts of enclaves across the state. Often, parishioners would buy a large plot of land that also allowed the construction of a school, meeting hall, and home for the priest. With the buildings in place, parishioners could focus on their faith by attending religious services and enjoying the camaraderie of numerous holiday seasons. Chief among these religious celebrations are Christmas, Easter, and St. Sava Day, while Palm Sunday, St. George's Day, and weddings each have their own significance in the community.

Of religious holidays, St. Sava Day remains a uniquely Serbian occasion that commemorates the patron saint of the country. Saint Sava was the youngest son of King Stephan I, who in the twelfth century founded the first Serbian state. Before his death in 1236, Saint Sava built two monasteries, founded the independent Serbian Orthodox Church, and wrote the nation's first constitution. These achievements propelled Saint Sava to the forefront of Serbian heroes, a position shared by Prince Lazar, who was martyred and beatified after the 1389 Battle of Kosovo. In modern Serbia the 269 foot tall

Saint Sava Cathedral, completed in 1989, dominates the skyline of Belgrade. After nearly a century of construction it is one of ten largest churches in the world, which seats 10,000 people and contains the remains of both Saint Sava and Prince Lazar, the two greatest heroes of Serbian history.[79]

This celebration actually emerged from a pre-Christian tradition to venerate family gods. As society transitioned into Christianity, saints replaced the pantheon of gods that people worshipped. The leader of the new Serbian Church, Saint Sava, forbade blood sacrifices and introduced Greek Orthodox religious symbols such as the candle (*vostanica*), wheat (*koljivo*), and bread (*kolač*) to celebrate the life, struggles, and resurrection of Jesus Christ. Since all life has been born from seed, the wheat grain came to symbolize both the body of Christ and Holy Mother, along with the veneration of the populations' main food crop. Thus, Saint Sava Day celebrations revolve around the blessing of wheat and breaking bread with family and friends because, "God helps him who celebrates his Slava" (*Ko Slavu slavi, njemu i Bog pomaze*).[80]

Serbian's have a great deal of diversity concerning when they celebrate Saint Sava Day (*Krsna Slava*), along with several aspects of the actual observance. Traditionally, a family will have their own patron such as St. Nicholas, St. John, St. George, St. Elijah, or Archangel Michael. The choice of saints usually descends through male lines and is usually adopted by women after they marry into the family. On or near the name day of their family's saint, the head of household will invite family and friends to their homes for the ceremony.

In a typical observance, a family will either bring a special Patron Saint's Cake to church for a public blessing or invite the priest to their home for a private service. In either case, the family will also have a bowl of cooked wheat sweetened with honey (*koljivo*), a book (*citulja*) with the names of deceased family members, an icon of their patron saint, lit candles, and wine laid out on a table. During a private ceremony, the priest begins by burning incense and reading the names of both living and dead family members, who are then offered prayers. He first cuts the cake crossways to symbolize the crucifixion, pours a small amount of wine over the cake, then blesses and kisses it three times. The cake is then passed to family members, who also kiss it before handing it back to the priest, who in turns breaks off small pieces for the family to eat. This commemorates both the living and dead family members, along with Saint Sava and all of the other deceased patron saints. The sweetened wheat represents the unity of the Orthodox faithful and their separation from other religious faiths. It is offered as a humble sacrifice to God in gratitude for the many blessings bestowed upon the family.[81]

Once the ceremony concludes, the feasting begins, with the sweetened wheat being passed in patriarchal order, starting with the eldest male of the family and ending with the youngest female guest. Each recipient makes the sign of the cross and eats a small spoonful of the *koljivo* in honor of the family. Then the first course of hors-d'oeuvres and brandy (*schlivovitz*) will be offered, followed by a succession of traditional Serbian food and liberal amounts of wines and spirits. Often, men will serve drinks while women spend the day preparing food and laying out the banquet for everyone to enjoy. Some favorite dishes are smoked ham, roast pork or lamb, sausage (*cevapcici*), and cabbage rolls (*sarma*) filled with meat. Plus a variety of cheeses (*Pule, Kajmak,* or *Pirot*), salads, breads, and desserts are also consumed in prodigious quantities. Music, singing, and dancing frequently accompany the meal. Moreover, people love to tell stories or personal anecdotes, often "salted" to produce a laugh. A myriad of discussions often ensue, although it is considered bad form to either drink too much or make disparaging remarks. In recent decades the celebration has changed in America as more non-Orthodox guests are invited to partake in a uniquely Serbian religious celebration. Nevertheless, St. Sava Day remains a central feature in the reaffirmation of faith and family.[82]

The celebration of Easter also plays a major role in the religious lives of Serbian families. The forty days leading to Easter are referred to as the Great Lent. During this period of general fasting, individuals are encouraged to reflect on their lives and devise ways to address any personal shortcomings. At the same time, people should make a greater effort to help others, attend church regularly, and read the Bible or other religious texts, but refrain from disparaging others or boasting of personal achievements. During the last two weeks before Easter Sunday, Serbs stop eating any meats, and in the final week they also exclude all dairy products. The last seven days are called Easter Week, which has a series of separate celebrations on Holy Thursday, Good Friday, and the Easter service. Families will keep a golden loaf of bread (*Artos*) in commemoration of Christ that will be eaten in church after a blessing by the priest on St. Thomas Sunday.[83]

In preparation for Easter, Serbs frequently make eggs by decoratively scratching patterns in the shell with a sharp blade and dyeing them in a variety of colors. The first egg completed is called the "Protector of the House" (*Cuvarkucca*) and kept near the family icon until St. Georges Day, which comes a few days after Easter.[84] Red is a popular color because it usually represents the blood of Christ as he redeemed the world, while the egg itself symbolizes the resurrection and the possibility of new life. With the arrival of Easter Sunday, the family attends church services and returns home to celebrate the end of fasting with a large meal consisting of the same types of traditional food consumed on St. Sava Day. A popular alternative, especially on a sunny day, is for the family to pack a picnic basket on Saturday, bring it to Easter church services, and then eat the meal outdoors as a pleasant family gathering.

Christmas (*Bozich*) celebrations have also changed over time to fit the modern world. Traditional Serbians celebrate Christmas on January 7th, but the devout may begin fasting as early as November 28th in order to cleanse their bodies of impurities. During the forty days leading up to Christmas, individuals refrain from eating meat, dairy, poultry, and eggs. For the less devout, the fast begins on January 6th in preparation for the Christmas Eve feast (*Posna Vecera*). As a fasting day, the Christmas Eve (*Badnji Dan*) dinner features various recipes that emphasize lentils, vegetables, dried fruit, and fish, which are allowed during the fasting period. These are typically served on small plates through multiple courses. Along with food there is an accompanying ceremony.

The male head of the family and his eldest son head into nearby forests in search of a yule log (*badnjak*) from an oak tree with leaves still attached. The log is either brought back whole or cut into three pieces to represent the Holy Trinity, and then brought individually into the house by the father. A family member then places the boughs into the hearth while the father and son exchange the formal greeting of "Good evening and happy Christmas Eve."[85] This ceremony is done to emulate the fire Joseph made in the stable to warm his wife, Mary, and newborn son, Jesus. It also symbolizes the suffering of Christ for humanity, along with the light and truth that radiated from Christ.[86] Several generations of females, who have been standing outdoors, come inside and spread straw on the floor, clucking like a chicken and chicks to symbolize family unity. The straw is placed near the table with a candle

Figure 5. Parishioners hold aloft badjnaks (oak tree branches laden with fruit and bedecked with ribbons) outside of the Ravanica Serbian Orthodox Church during a Christmas celebration. Father Miodrag Mijatovich stands at center. Walter P. Reuther Library, Archives of Labor and Urban Affairs, Wayne State University.

and possibly the family icon. With the completion of the ritual, the family can then eat the Christmas Eve dinner. Afterwards, the father and grandfather throw walnuts into the room's corners to form a cross. However, in modern times cutting trees and dropping hay do not work well in urban settings. Instead, many will simply buy an oak wreath and hang it from the front door. Others may add candles or an icon, but the Christmas Eve feast remains largely the same.

Early the next morning, the family will attend Christmas services and then return home to start greeting visitors, who will be stopping by for the next three days. The person invited to arrive first (*polozajnik*) is the honored guest for the day. This begins a ritual where the host kisses the guest, stating "Christ is born" (*Hristos Se Rodi*), which is answered with "Indeed He is born" (*Voistino Se Rodi*).[87] That is followed by the guest pulling the burning yule log from the fire and wishing the host family good fortune in the coming year. The Christmas dinner usually features a whole roasted pig (*Pechenitsa*) as the main course, plus a special cake (*Chesnica*). The Christmas cake is either made of flour or a nut pastry, with a special coin baked inside. When the cake is cut, the person who has the coin will have an especially lucky year.

Along with the positive attributes of communal festivals, Serbs also endured a religious schism between the official State Church in Belgrade and the local dioceses in North America that lasted for nearly thirty years. The conflict split both families and communities, leading to a new wave of church construction in the 1960s and 1970s, as individuals demanded places of worship that conformed to their political and religious beliefs. While traumatic, the era of conflict also illustrated a feature in the Americanization process that occurred in other ethnic communities with national churches. Namely, that the break from the homeland church allowed the formation of an independent church without political implications, which reflects the separation of politics and religion, an ingrained aspect of American society.

Serbian Orthodoxy in America had its origins in 1894, when Fr. Sebastian Dabovich built the first church in Jackson, California. During the early phase of religious development, officials of the much larger and more established Russian Orthodox Church appointed an administrator to oversee the Serbian population. For Detroit's Serbian population, the year 1915 marked the beginning of an independent church when Bishop Varnava, while on a missionary assignment in Detroit, offered a Christmas service in a rented building. Within two years, property was purchased across the street from the rented building and work began on the first Serbian Orthodox church in the city, along with a school and residence for the parish priest. By 1934, the congregation completed the new St. Lazarus Serbian Orthodox Church, also called "Ravanica," to commemorate the final resting place of St. Lazar, hero of the Serbian people. It was finally completed after the congregation struggled to pay off the mortgage during the economic turbulence of the Great Depression. The new church became a center for Serbian life in Detroit and neighboring Windsor, Canada, until additional churches were built in the region.[88] The church maintained its vibrancy by working with young people, second-generation Serbian immigrants who had never been to Europe and had learned about their history and culture from parents and neighbors.

In order to attract young members into the Serbian Orthodox Church, an issue of uncertainty because of American religious freedom, parishioners

Figure 6. Saint Lazarus Cathedral, Detroit, Michigan. Paul Bielich, Saint Lazarus Cathedral, Detroit, Ravanica Church Archive.

had to make joining the community an attractive alternative to the Catholic or Protestant denominations that dominated in the United States. In Detroit, the Ravanica church community organized the St. Lazar Club of Young Serbs. The youth group gained respect within the enclave by raising funds to build an even larger and more ornate church than the one currently in use. They also created a church bulletin, the *Voice of Ravanica,* which was one of the first in the region. In 1935, the executive board of the Serb National Federation (SNF) decided to promote English in their lodge proceedings, so they changed bylaws to include both languages, but English would dominate during meetings.

Additionally, the SNF newspaper *American Srbobran* introduced an English-language section in 1939 to help sustain readership among younger generations in the community.[89] The newspaper provided advice on how to build English-language lodges in Serbian communities throughout the nation. They suggested that individuals "Go to some intelligent boy or girl in your colony" for leadership and encourage them to gather other teens over sixteen years old, regardless of gender, to volunteer their time to the endeavor. The volunteers were supposed to collect the names and addresses of prospective members, then mail out invitations. The directions also recommended that volunteers gather enough application forms from the federation and hire an inexpensive doctor capable of conducting physical exams on the candidates to ensure their suitability in the organization. Once all the details had been completed, the volunteers were instructed to contact an older member of the organization, who knew the bylaws, to provide advice during the initial meeting. When twelve or more members had been gathered, they should hold elections for officials, and then they would become an official lodge in the Serbian community.[90]

Another way Serbs maintained their cultural heritage in America was through sports. Competitions helped to unite local populations, while national championships helped to maintain the social cohesiveness of far-flung Serbian enclaves that dominated western and midwestern states. While European sports such as soccer dominated among first-generation immigrants, their children preferred American games. Beginning in 1935, Serbian church and social groups began holding national bowling and basketball tournaments. The tradition has continued to this day and remains an important aspect of Serbian American communities.

During this early phase of church and community development, as the number of individual parishes increased, the need for more centralized ways of dealing with religious issues became apparent. In 1921, an independent Serbian Diocese of North America and Canada was formed in Cleveland, Ohio. The new international Serbian Orthodox diocese came under the leadership of an immigrant from Podgorica, Montenegro, Bishop Mardary Uskokovich. Immediately, construction began outside Chicago, in Libertyville, on a new monastery and orphanage that would serve as the religious center of Serbian Orthodoxy in America. In 1935, Bishop Mardary died, paving the way for Bishop Dionisije Milivojevich to take over and lead the Serbian American population through the turbulence of the Second World War. However, Bishop Dionisije's staunch anticommunist stance quickly led to conflict within Serbian American communities, mirroring similar events taking place in Yugoslavia.

During the spring of 1941, Adolf Hitler unleashed his Nazi armies in a coordinated attack on Yugoslavia, with military assistance from Italy and Bulgaria. The overwhelming superiority of the fascist soldiers quickly conquered the country, forcing King Peter II Karađorđević to flee and join other exiled anti-Nazi governments in England. During the German occupation of Yugoslavia, two opposing factions emerged that fought not only the invaders, but each other as well. General Draža Mihailović commanded "Chetnik" forces loyal to the exiled king, while Josip Broz or "Tito" sought to defeat Nazi forces, depose the king, and form a communist government in the country with his Partizan army. Over the course of the war, American and British support gradually transitioned from Mihailović to Tito, who took a more active role in fighting Germans. These events culminated in the Partizans defeating the German army in 1944–1945, propelling Tito and his communists to power over the country and forcing Mihailović's army into exile, with many arriving in the United States after the war.

Serbian Americans followed the events in Yugoslavia with great interest, reading stories in a variety of newspapers. As the American government began to back Tito's Partizans over the king's Chetniks, Bishop Dionisije became more concerned about the possibility of a communist revolution seizing power in Yugoslavia. He then began an organized campaign to stop communist expansion in both Europe and America. In the United States, the bishop's position was criticized by clergy and the publishers of the Serbian American communist newspaper *Slobodna Rec* (Free Press) and in Chicago-area papers for English readers.[91] The constant barrage of abuse put the bishop on the defensive and helped to feed his anticommunist attitude.

In 1945, Bishop Dionisije, Louis Christopher of the Serb National Federation, along with Mitchell Duchich, president of the Serbian National Defense Council of America, sent a petition to President Roosevelt asking him to abide by the Atlantic Charter, which stated that the United States sought to restore the prewar governments and borders in Europe. They also requested that Roosevelt reverse his position on Yugoslavia and support General Mihailović, who would overthrow Tito and create a free Serbia.[92] As Tito gained military strength and political power, Serbian American papers, such as *The American Serb,* began to report on communist atrocities. In a December 1945 edition, Tito's Partizans were accused of gruesomely murdering sixty intellectuals near the village of Doli, in Slovenia.[93] Similar stories helped to turn popular opinion against Tito and added to the overall fear in the United States of communist world conquest.

In Detroit, the Serbian community organized to help incoming refugees fleeing the communist takeover in Yugoslavia. Father Miodrag Mijatovich, who had led the Ravanica congregation since 1943, welcomed 350 refugees to his parish after the war.[94] The rapid change in population contributed to the need to build a bigger church. In 1948, planning had begun for an expanded Ravanica facility in Detroit, modeled on a church built by St. Lazar near the town of Chuprija, in Southern Serbia. Before construction could begin, the current church had to be sold and funds gathered to support the expensive development. In conjunction with the fundraising, an edition of *American Serb Life* reported that Dr. Stanley Papich, a chiropractor and choir member, was leading the fundraising movement. His efforts resulted in the collection of $27,500 toward the construction project. However, the article also noted that former servicemen had chased all the "Reds" out of Detroit[95]—thus indicating that the Detroit Serbian community had been actively participating in anticommunist activities after the arrival of the war refugees, and therefore church members were not part of the immigrant communist movement in the United States.

Nevertheless, the Serbian refugees soon joined forces with Bishop Dionisije, who was already an ardent anticommunist, thereby creating an opposition movement to Marshal Tito in the United States. Unfortunately, their stance also caused a rift within Serbian American communities. Dionisije and the exiles rejected any form of cooperation with Serbian Orthodox Church officials in Belgrade. They considered the current church officials to be communist sympathizers for not actively working to overthrow Tito's government. In return, Patriarch German viewed Bishop Dionisije as a political opportunist, more interested in personal aggrandizement than in the religious needs of his parishioners.[96] As a result of the significant differences, parishes dominated by established and second-generation Serbs maintained positive relations with Belgrade's church officials. These Serbian Americans remained focused on purely religious issues and not political intrigues unfolding in Yugoslavia.[97] In contrast, Bishop Dionisije and his supporters formed the Serbian National Committee as an anticommunist organization, with a goal of using church officials to mediate differences between royalists and communists. When Tito visited the United States in 1963, Dionisije and

Serbian National Committee members staged protests where they carried signs while also burning and hanging effigies of the communist dictator in front of large crowds.

The embarrassing situation not only forced Tito to cancel the rest of his American tour and return to Yugoslavia, but set off a chain of events culminating in a schism in the Serbian Orthodox Church. Events began to unfold when Tito arrived in Belgrade. He turned to Patriarch German, leader of the Serbian Church, who quickly ordered the creation of three new dioceses in North America and began the process to dismiss Dionisije from his position in the church.[98] Patriarch German dispatched Bishops Hristostom and Visarian, along with the Very Reverend Mladenovich to America, where they began an investigation of allegations of personal impropriety and misuse of church property leveled against the American bishop.[99] The committee formally concluded that Bishop Dionisije had not followed the directives of the Holy Council of Bishops and Synod; therefore, he was defrocked and excommunicated from the Serbian Orthodox Church. A response came from the Church National Assembly of the American-Canadian Diocese that asked the Patriarchate to reconsider their decision concerning Dionisije and the creation of new dioceses. The Patriarchate responded by ruling that the Church National Assembly was an illegal organization, which resulted in Bishop Dionisije and the American-Canadian Diocese officially breaking from the Serbian Church.

Leaders of the Free Church claimed 20 of 59 parishes in America that comprised 150,000 families.[100] The schism quickly divided both families and communities, as individuals had to decide which group posed the greatest threat: the alleged communists among second-generation immigrants, or the parasynagogues who led the newly arrived immigrants. The combative situation set off a new wave of Serbian Orthodox Church construction in the United States as each side sought houses of worship that also suited personal political beliefs. Four major religious centers emerged during the 1960s as a result of the breakup. Bishop Dionisije retained the organizational name of Serbian Diocese of North America and Canada, along with control of the St. Sava Monastery, in Illinois. Serbian Church officials divided North America into three dioceses. The new Midwest American Diocese, under Bishop Firmilian, nominally operated out of Libertyville. In actuality, he worked in

Milwaukee and later in Chicago because Bishop Dionisije occupied the St. Sava Monastery. Bishop Lastavica led the Eastern American and Canadian Diocese from Detroit, while Bishop Grigorije took control of the Western American Diocese in Alhambra, California.

In Detroit, Bishop Dionisije struggled to build up his independent church and congregations. Protracted legal battles over church property led to several victories in which the courts sided with the majority number of parishioners over which side retained control over contested buildings. In April 1966 the Illinois Appellate Court ruled that Serbian Patriarch German had no power to dissolve the American Diocese without the consent of the parishioners. The court stated that the constitution and bylaws of the Serbian Diocese of North America and Canada conferred power on their bishop, and not the church leaders in Belgrade.[101] The ruling also stated that pro-Belgrade parishioners had to leave the independent churches, while rejecting all claims by the three new bishops. The decisions conformed to similar findings in earlier court cases concerning the breakup of Protestant national churches operating in the United States. The May 1966 rulings encouraged the independent churches to remove traditionalists from their congregations who still followed Patriarch German.[102] A few months later, in December 1966, Patriarch German excommunicated all members of the independent church. Bishop Dionisije and his followers immediately rejected the ruling because they no longer recognized the authority of the Serbian Orthodox Church.[103]

In Detroit, the Very Reverend Miodrag Mijatovic of the "Ravanica" Church would play an instrumental role in ministering to parishioners loyal to Patriarch German. He continued with plans to build a larger Saint Lazarus Ravanica Church complex in Detroit.[104] Patriarch German rewarded the congregation by sending religious relics from St. Lazarus, along with a special blessing for the Serbian people who toiled in Detroit's factories.[105] In the 1950s, Fr. Mijatovich had helped to fund and build the St. George the Great Martyr Church in the city of Monroe, just south of Detroit. Fr. Matejic led the congregation through the breakup, while maintaining a close working relationship with Fr. Mijatovich.[106] The support for smaller local churches continued into the 1980s, with the creation of St. Petka. Most of the members came from Vratnice, Bosnia, and regularly attended services at Ravanica. When they wanted their own church, officials not only approved the organization, they brought in a priest from Vratnice to serve as parish priest.[107]

Figure 7. His Grace Rt. Rev. Dr. Bishop Sava; His Grace Rt. Rev. Bishop Firmilian; His Grace Rt. Rev. Bishop Gregory. Paul Bielich, Saint Lazarus Cathedral, Detroit, Ravanica Church Archive.

Bishop Dionisije not only brought in new priests from Yugoslavia, but he also began the construction of new churches in the Detroit area. Early on, a lack of funds forced parishioners to use their own homes for religious services. For example, the Holy Ascension Church in Ecorse, Michigan, began in the converted parlor of Vuko Dragovich's home. By 1968, work had been completed on a formal Orthodox church building and a Serbian Hall where people could hold meetings, dances, or celebrations. Both Fr. Uglesha Yelich and later Fr. Milan Popovich became popular leaders at the new church.[108] Construction also began on the new St. Stephen of Dechani Church, located only a few blocks north of Ravanica in Detroit. In September 1965, Bishop Dionisije broke ground on the $200,000 project that included the church, hall, and school complex.[109] Two years later, the bishop consecrated the completed religious center accompanied by Walter Vukas, Wayne Felbarth, and Mrs. Vojnovich of the Serbian Circle of Women. The officials took the opportunity offered by the momentous occasion to welcome several new parishioners who had been expelled from Ravanica Church for supporting the dissident bishop.[110]

Throughout the 1960s, the Ravanica and Dechani factions maintained tense relations, frequently interspersed with criticisms based on their divergent political and religious beliefs. For example, in 1965 approximately eight hundred of Dionisije's parishioners gathered in Chicago to commemorate the communist takeover of Yugoslavia and support President Johnson's war on communism in Vietnam. They further denounced anyone who supported Yugoslavia's dictator Marshal Tito or Patriarch German.[111] The following year in the *Diocesan Observer,* a paper that supported Bishop Dionisije, referred to a trip by Serbian American singers to Yugoslavia as treason.[112] In 1968, a similar trip to Yugoslavia by Ravanica singers also met with derision in the *Diocesan Observer,* which described the event as disloyalty for giving gold to Tito after the president asked Americans to stop unnecessary foreign travel in communist countries.[113]

By the 1970s and 1980s, changes began to affect relations between the two factions, gradually moving them toward reconciliation. The Supreme Court ruled that Patriarch German not only had a right to defrock Bishop Dionisije but also to retain the St. Sava Monastery, which occurred in 1979 after further legal wrangling. In the same year, Bishop Dionisije died and was replaced by Bishop Iriney, who took over the newly renamed Free American Canadian Diocese. When Marshal Tito died in 1981, communism ended in Yugoslavia, thus negating one of the primary reasons behind the creation of the Free Church. Attempts were made in the 1980s to reconcile the factions, but neither side could agree on what to do about the defrocked clergy, hierarchy, and property of the Free Church in America. Furthermore, Bishop Iriney could not overcome internal dissension from anticommunist organizations that supported the church. These groups included the Serbian

National Defense, the Chetnik Movement (Ravna Gora), the Association of the Royal Yugoslav Army, the Association of Serbian Fighters, the Serbian Cultural Club, and the Serbian People's University.[114] Instead of reconciling, the Free Church established ties with anticommunist factions in Serbia, Montenegro, Bosnia, and Karlovac.[115]

In 1991, the death of Patriarch German and the election of Patriarch Pavle opened the door to the reunification of the Serbian Orthodox Church. By then, much of the visceral anger that led to the split had died with the elderly combatants. Younger members of both factions no longer felt the need to argue over communism, especially after the fall of the Berlin Wall in 1989 and the 1991 downfall of the Soviet Union. Patriarch Pavle entrusted a professor from the Belgrade Theological College, the Very Reverend Archimandrite, Dr. Atanasije Jevtic with investigating the schism and formulating a reconciliation plan. Professor Jevtic suggested that they merge the four dioceses already existing in North America, including the clergy and church hierarchy. All priests defrocked for disobedience should be rehabilitated and recognized as members of the Serbian Orthodox Church. He also recommended that representative bodies made up of Free Church parishioners be included in negotiations.[116]

Using these ideas as a basis for further negotiations, in April 1991 Patriarch Pavle invited Bishop Iriney and representatives from the Free Church to Belgrade. During the ensuing talks, both sides concluded that the Free Church would recognize the authority of the Serbian Orthodox Patriarchate, accept a name change to the Serbian Orthodox Metropolitanate of New Gracanica, but retain control over their church properties. Deceased and present clergy, including Bishop Dionisije, were rehabilitated and brought into the Serbian Church. The end result was that the rift had been sealed, and the new organization has been divided into four eparcies, including Canada, Western America, Mid-Western America, and Eastern America.

Music

During the centuries of Ottoman rule over the Serbian people in Europe, religion, literature, and music helped to maintain Serbian culture through the turbulent period. In the nineteenth and twentieth centuries, as Serbians began to arrive in the United States, arts and literature continued to instill generations of immigrants with nostalgic feelings for their mother country. Homesick immigrants turned to their lyric and literary roots for solace, after toiling for hours in the factories, farms, mines, and lumber mills that constituted Michigan's industrial revolution.[117] Their shared traditions found homes in the Serbian Halls built adjacent to their churches, and in bars and clubs that the immigrants frequented in their communities. Inside the walls, immigrants found shelter from the hectic pace of American life. They spoke their native language, read Serbian American newspapers, and consumed plum brandy, a traditional drink among Serbian people. With a sense of comfort, the immigrants could sing or dance without fear of outside interference.

Many of the songs the Serbian immigrants performed were written during the Ottoman occupation and formed part of the nationalistic tradition that ultimately resulted in nineteenth-century Serbian independence. The musical styles and topics followed gender lines. Women practiced lyrical singing. They sang about their daily lives, universal and enduring experiences—such

Love's Trial

During the First World War, Maximilian A. Mugge compiled *Serbian Folk Songs, Fairy Tales and Proverbs* to help gain public support for an allied government. This is one of the limited number of books on Serbian traditional literature available in English.

Love's Trial

Thirty sturdy fellows from Cetinje
Seated near the cool and quiet river,
Quaffed their wine and teased the pretty maiden
Who supplied their ever empty goblets.
Bolder than the rest, some tried to kiss her.
But the maiden from Cetinje told them,
"Though a waitress to you all, my fellows,
Sweetheart am I but to him who ventures
For my sake to swim this mighty river;
Let him take his sword and all this armour;
Furthermore, I wish that on his shoulders
He shall wear this precious velvet mantle.
Thus from bank to bank the hero-swimmer
Cross the river, and on his returning
I will be his faithful wife for ever!"

as the life cycle of individuals and community, births, deaths, family relationships, or seasonal work—that made up peasant life. In contrast, men sang heroic ballads that promoted nationalism.[118]

The male singer traditionally used a single-string fiddle, held with the knees and played with a bow, called a *gusle*. The singer or *guslari* had to learn a repertoire of thirty folk songs, each lasting seven or eight hours, to be considered an accomplished musician. The number of songs represented each day of the month, which was the length of time a singer could be expected to entertain a community. The songs had approximately 25,000 lines, made up of ten syllables.[119] The *guslari* typically altered the number of lines

But for one, the thirty valiant warriors
Looked shameface'dly into their goblets.
He, however, dared her, leaped up quickly,
Donned his armour, took his sword, the mantle
Heavy as a coronation garment,
Dived into the river, swam across it,
Touched the other bank just with his sword-point;
Then returned, but all at once—went under!
Not that suddenly his strength had failed him,
No! he swam below the water's surface
That he might find out his love's devotion.
When the maiden from Cetinje saw it,
With a cry of anguish she ran forwards
Straight into the river to her lover
Radoiza. Then the daring swimmer
Grasped her firmly by the hands, and with her
Gained the land where his companions cheered him.
Soon he led away with him the maiden,
Now the mistress of his white-hued homestead.

or syllables to fit the mood of the crowd. Further changes could be made through lengthening or shortening dramatic stories, even changing details that listeners could compare to other singers. These songs usually addressed battles, horses, and heroic figures in Serbia's past. Others contained more mundane issues including messages, letters, disguises, weddings. The topic of love also received a great deal of attention, whether unrequited or fulfilled, abandoned or betrayed. However, sitting through an eight-hour concert was not practical in American life. Immigrants had to work set hours in an industrial society; therefore the Serbian Americans did not have the same free time found in agricultural cultures, especially during winter months. These factors contributed to the unpopularity of musical epic folktales as popular entertainment.

Instead of epic folktales, immigrants turned to the much more upbeat tamburitza music from their mother country for popular culture. The practice of combining several long-necked lutes (*tamburitza*) into a band started in the mid-nineteenth century in areas of Slovonia and Vojvodina.[120] Other traditional instruments that could be included in a band were accordions, a shepherd's flute (*svirala*), or bagpipes (*gajde*). Because Slovonia and Vojvodina were relatively isolated regions, with little outside contact, other Serbian populations were unfamiliar with the music until they arrived in the United States. In the heterogeneous Serbian American enclaves, tamburitza music quickly supplanted other forms of traditional music. Furthermore, Serbians considered their music to be superior to jazz, which Anglo-Americans preferred. A Serbian critic denigrated jazz by calling it "a prostitution of music" made up of "rhythmical noises."[121] The rapid ascendancy of tamburitza music also led to changes in the genre.

Serbians continued to play their traditional songs until after the First World War, when governmental immigration restrictions cut off the supply of music emerging in Yugoslavia, along with immigrants. Around 1924, the situation led to the emergence of a strictly Serbian American version of the genre. Along with the new style, two types of tamburitza bands emerged in Serbian communities. The first were small, informal groups of musicians, playing in local bars or among friends. Much larger and formalized orchestras emerged a short time later. The bands or orchestras differed from the informal groups by touring regionally instead of locally. They also played a greater variety of music, including polkas, waltzes, overtures, and marches.[122] The bands were usually made up of males belonging to the same extended family from several generations. Groups such as the Crlenica Brothers and the Popovich Brothers, along with the Dokich Dynasty and the Kachars all became household names.

Generally, women did not play in tamburitza bands, although girls occasionally played in youth groups until they married. However, during the Second World War, with most of the men gone, women began to form their own groups. After the war, some of the male tamburitza bands also added women as vocalists to provide more range in their music. Gorica Popovich and Alexandra Djordjevich both started their careers in Detroit, but Gorica

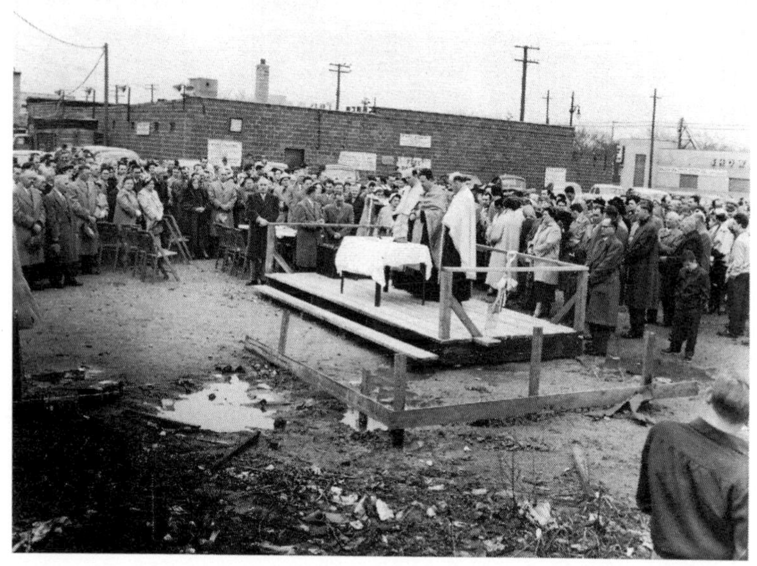

Figure 8. The 1952 groundbreaking ceremony for the new American Serbian Memorial Hall in Detroit. Paul Bielich, Saint Lazarus Cathedral, Detroit, Ravanica Church Archive.

moved to California and sang with the Veseli Seljaci orchestra. Olga Kolman also had several hit records during the 1940s, playing with a variety of musicians and orchestras. While she had a relatively short career, Olga maintained numerous ardent fans.[123] The Trivanovich Sisters, from Cleveland, Ohio, became one of the most popular groups between the 1940s and 1960s, when family life finally superseded touring, at least temporarily. After 1996, they reformed as the Šarena Tamburitza Orchestra, which still tours Serbian American communities throughout the Midwest.[124]

For the Serbian population in Detroit, the tamburitza musicians gathered in famous venues such as Jim's Cabaret, Convoy's, the Yugoslav Palace, Sofi's, the Butcher's Club, and the Blue Danube.[125] Most were centered around the Serbian enclave on Russell Street, which stretched north for six blocks from Hancock to Ferry Street and was bordered by Rivard and Riopelle to the east and west. On one side stood a Polish neighborhood and on the other, African Americans.[126] However, urban growth has turned most of the area into a series of businesses and parking lots. Nevertheless, one

Figure 9. An exhibition of Serbian folk dancing at Detroit's Masonic Temple. Walter P. Reuther Library, Archives of Labor and Urban Affairs, Wayne State University.

of the foremost modern tamburitza players to emerge from the area was Alexander "Sanda" Pavlovich. His family owned the Blue Danube, which gave him a ready location to show his talents. Not that he really needed it though, because Sanda showed musical talent from an early age, playing his first concert at fourteen years old, for a wedding. From there he went on to join the Slavulj Orchestra, and in 1965 he organized the Lira Orchestra.[127] Their music gained widespread popularity after being featured on Detroit's WJBK radio station, which played ethnic music for the city's diverse immigrant populations.

Along with bars and nightclubs, Serbian churches, halls, weddings, holidays, or Sunday afternoon fairs have all been popular venues for the tamburitza bands. In a typical celebration, children begin playing songs they learned while practicing their instruments. Afterwards, the adults take over, playing dance music to entertain the crowd. A popular dance style is called a circle (*kolo*), which includes several variations such as the *šest, malo kolo, kokunješte,* and *žikino.*[128] In a kolo dance, a circle of men and women join hands in front of themselves at shoulder height, with their elbows slightly bent. With their bodies held rigidly upright, individuals move their feet front then back, sideways, while either walking, running, or hopping. The dance begins when participants begin moving their hands up and down in a wave motion. Each circle has a dance leader who then chooses the steps, rhythms, tempo, direction, and conclusion of the dance. At certain points the leader will enter the circle, demonstrate their skill, then hand it over to the next dancer.[129] A version within the church or hall dance was called a bachelor (*becar*), where men gathered to sing nineteenth-century nationalistic songs. While women could attend, they were separated from the men. These types of parties could last for several hours and provided generations of Serbian Americans with inexpensive entertainment.

The Serbian American tamburitza bands owe a debt of gratitude to the pioneering spirit of George Kachar, Matt Gouze, and Vladimir M. Lugonja. Among them, George Kachar had the distinction of training the first generation of Serbian American tamburitza players. This work began during the early twentieth century, in a small Colorado mining town. While training numerous young men, his best students were four brothers named Eli, Adam, Teddy, and Marko Popovich, who founded the group the Popovich Brothers. They continually toured Serbian communities throughout America from the 1920s until the 1990s. They even played for President Eisenhower and at the White House for President Clinton's inaugural ceremony.[130] Along with playing innumerable concerts, the Popovich Brothers also trained a generation of musicians who would continue the musical tradition. The formalization of the new musical style began in 1937 with Matt Gouze, who established the Duquesne University Tamburitzans in Pittsburg, Pennsylvania. The group had a dual role, offering formal training in a university setting and becoming role models for several generations of South Slavic musicians.[131]

Vladimir M. Lugonja (Vlajko) played a critical role not only in the tamburitza movement, but also in forming Serbian American choral groups. Lugonja was born in Chemerno, Herzegovina, during 1898, and in 1907 moved to Chicago, where he became involved in the foundation of the American tamburitza movement. Lugonja eventually followed his sister to Detroit in the 1920s and helped with her with a family restaurant. However, he missed his earlier musical career and helped to form Detroit's first male choir, named "Philip Visnich." In 1930, he moved on to found Detroit's Ravanica Church Choir.[132] The group's motto was "He Who Sings Thinks No Evil" (Ko Peva, Zlo Ne Misli).[133] This expanded into the Serbian Singing Federation in the 1930s, which helped raise the parishioners' morale during the Great

Depression. He began recruiting support for the organization by writing a series of articles in the newspaper *Srbobran* and speaking with regional choral groups and other associations that might be able to support the program.

By early 1931, Lugonja had called a national conference to create a Serbian Singing Federation. Five groups responded to the invitation, including two from Chicago, with Gary, Youngstown, and Detroit each sending one chorus. Officials from each choral group then elected Petar Sekulovich to be the organization's president, with the headquarters in Lugonja's home in Detroit. The first national festival took place in 1936 at an Akron, Ohio, Memorial Day celebration. Sixteen groups arrived in Akron, including one from Yugoslavia. The festival proved so popular that the city's hotels filled to capacity and individuals could only find room to sleep at local police stations and hospitals.[134] As the choirs became more popular, more groups joined the organization, leading to thirty individual bodies in the federation before the Second World War. At the festivals, early competitors vied for championship cups, but this practice soon ended. Instead, the choir members competed for honor and demonstrating their religious conviction. During the Second World War years, choir membership declined as members joined the military, went to work in factories, or helped gather relief parcels for Serbian refugees. Once hostilities ended, the singing resumed with the 1948 national festival held in Pittsburg, Pennsylvania.

In the postwar era, being picked as a soloist was a major honor for any singer invited to one of the many music festivals. A prewar tradition of sending Serbian American singers to Yugoslavia continued, despite political differences between the United States and Tito's communist government. For example, during America's 1976 Bicentennial celebrations, special performances of Ljubomir Bosnjakovich's folk music "Albanska Golgota" took place in Milwaukee, Wisconsin, and Steubenville, Ohio. The music extolled the bravery of Serbian soldiers and civilians forced to flee the onslaught of the Austro-Hungarian army during the First World War; thus the piece was another example of Serbian music promoting nationalism. During the same year, the Serbian Singing Federation celebrated the career of Vladimir M. Lugonja with a gala and grand testimonial in Detroit. His contributions to music had also helped to preserve Serbian identity through several generations of Americanization, thereby guaranteeing him a respected position in Serbian American history.

Lugonja died in 1977 and was buried at the Orthodox monastery in Libertyville, Illinois. However, his organization continues to thrive and preserve traditional Serbian music in America. The Serbian Singing Federation purchased a building to serve as a museum, which holds the largest collection of Serbian music in the United States.[135] The federation and museum continue the work Lugonja began in the 1930s, for the next several generations of Serbian Americans.

Conclusion

The story of Michigan's Serbian populations contains both typical and unique elements compared with the other immigrant populations in the state. Serbian émigrés left their homelands because of political, economic, and social pressures. When they arrived in Michigan they entered a period of vibrant economic growth. The Serbian immigrants went to work and used their wages to establish a series of comfortable enclaves to live and raise their families. They built churches, schools, and halls to preserve and celebrate their traditions. Furthermore, the Serbian immigrants published their own newspapers that allowed individuals who did not speak English to learn about current events in Europe and America. At the same time, Serbs taught their children to speak English, so they too could prosper in their new homeland.

The children who became second-generation Serbian Americans also followed a typical pattern found in other immigrant groups. These individuals had one foot in American culture and the other in Serbian traditions. With loyalty split between two distinct communities, the second generation had to either compromise a variety of beliefs such as religious conviction, marriage rituals, and loyalty to the government, or completely adapt to one of their heritages. This confusing situation caused rifts between generations as parents sought to preserve their Serbian traditions, while their children wanted to emulate their American peers. Further discord came from political battles fought between capitalists and communists in Serbian enclaves. While the capitalists eventually won, the protracted fighting led many people to leave their traditional communities along with altering their religious convictions, which has reduced the number of people who view themselves as Serbian Americans over successive generations.

However, Serbian American communities also possess unique elements that have helped to preserve Serbian culture. Foremost, the Serbian Orthodox Church preserved a national identity over several centuries of military occupation by the Ottoman Empire. The church promoted nationalistic ideas through a shared sense of identity, reinforced through music and stories. In this way, church leaders have maintained a central role in every Serbian enclave. In Detroit, the Saint Lazarus Serbian Orthodox Cathedral emerged not only as the first Serbian church in the state, but also as a cultural and religious leader. Members of the congregation supported other Serbian enclaves as they sought to build their own churches. The Serbian Sisters and the United Serbian Women illustrate the positive role women played in community development. The members organized schools and summer camps to pass on traditions and educate future leaders among Serbian Americans. Their forethought and hard work have also preserved Serbian American national identity.

That identity survived the single most traumatic event in Serbian American history, the nearly thirty-year-long church schism that divided families and enclaves across the United States. The breakdown of national churches in America was quite common during the nineteenth and twentieth centuries. However, the Serbian Church's traditional role in maintaining national identity, even under a foreign government, made the division highly unusual for parishioners. The truly unique feature was not the schism itself, but the eventual reconciliation of the two parties after the particularly rancorous exchanges and protracted legal battles. The Serbian Orthodox Church ultimately proved its strength and endurance as a vehicle for national preservation by overcoming a major influence of Americanization, the breakdown of foreign national churches. This points to the continuity of Serbian influences and maintenance of a distinct Serbian American community in the United States for the foreseeable future.

Appendix 1

Famous Serbian Americans

Predrag Bjelac (June 30, 1962): Actor best known for his roles in *Harry Potter and the Goblet of Fire* and *The Chronicles of Narnia: Prince Caspian.*

Peter Bogdanovich (July 30, 1939): Noted Hollywood director, actor, and critic who won a Golden Globe Award for his movie *Paper Moon,* while his later film *Mask* was nominated for the Palme d'Or.

Ivan Boldirev (August 15, 1949): Played in the NHL from 1970 to 1985, ending his career with the Detroit Red Wings, after playing over 1,000 games.

Mike Brkovich (April 6, 1958): While actually born in Canada, Brkovich played basketball for the Michigan State University Spartans, helping them win the 1979 NCAA National Championship.

Louis "Lou" Cukelja (May 1, 1888–March 19, 1956): Cukelja served in the United States Marine Corps during the First World War. He won two Medals of Honor and three Silver Stars for bravery in battle, plus the French Legion of Honor during fighting on the Western Front.

Vlade Divac (February 3, 1968): Played in the NBA from 1989 to 2005 for teams such as the Los Angeles Lakers and the Sacramento Kings. Divac played over a thousand games, was selected for the NBA Hall of Fame, and in 2009 the Kings retired his jersey.

Michael Glusac (July 28, 1930): Earned a degree from Wayne State University

Law School, served as mayor of Highland Park, and as an executive for the Chrysler Corporation.

Milla Jovovich (December 17, 1975): Model and actress, best known for her recurring role in the *Resident Evil* films and her role in *The Fifth Element.*

Lene Lovich (March 30, 1949): A Detroit-born singer and actress whose song "Lucky Number," released in 1978, topped the charts.

"Pistol" Pete Maravich (June 22, 1947–January 5, 1988): Played in the NBA from 1970 to 1980, remembered for long-range shooting and as one of the best players in the league. The Utah Jazz and the New Orleans Hornets retired his jersey.

Catherine Oxenberg (September 22, 1961): Starred in the television program *Dynasty* and numerous other movies; she is also the daughter of Princess Elizabeth of Yugoslavia.

Mitchell "Pejic" Paige (August 31, 1918–November 15, 2003): While serving in the Marine Corps during the Second World War, he won the Congressional Medal of Honor for repelling a Japanese attack during a critical phase of fighting on Guadalcanal.

Sonja Petrović (February 18, 1989): Women's National Basketball Association player for the Chicago Sky.

Michael Pupin (October 9, 1858–March 12, 1935): Physicist, chemist, and inventor who revolutionized long-distance telecommunications. He also won the 1924 Pulitzer Prize for his autobiography *From Immigrant to Inventor.*

Mladen Sekulovich (March 22, 1912–July 1, 2009): Better known as the actor Karl Malden, who won an Academy Award for his role in *A Streetcar Named Desire.* He starred in *On the Waterfront* and in the television series *The Streets of San Francisco.*

Lance Peter Sijan (April 13, 1942–January 22, 1968): Served in the Air Force as a fighter pilot during the Vietnam War. After being shot down, he stopped rescue efforts to protect other aircrew. Sijan was captured and tortured by the North Vietnamese, eventually dying from a combination of injuries and neglect. President Ford posthumously awarded him the Congressional Medal of Honor.

Dušan "Charles" Simić (May 9, 1938): A Pulitzer Prize–winning poet for his work *The World Doesn't End* and selected as United States Poet Laureate. He also wrote *Unending Blues* and *Selected Poems.*

Pete Stoyanovich (April 28, 1967): From Dearborn Heights, he played in the NFL from 1989 to 2000 as a placekicker. He holds the record for longest field goal while playing for the Miami Dolphins.

Nikola Tesla (July 19, 1856–January 7, 1943): Helped to modernize the United States by developing Alternating Current (AC) electrical power. He started the Tesla Electric Company in 1887, and went on to make contributions in radio communications, x-rays, and laser technology.

Steve "Stojan" Tesich (September 29, 1942–July 1, 1996): Won the Best Screenplay Academy Award in 1979 for his movie *Breaking Away*. He wrote numerous plays and had a best-selling novel, *Karoo,* which has been translated into several languages.

Pete Vuckovich (October 27, 1952): Major League Baseball pitcher for the Chicago White Soxs, Toronto Blue Jays, and Saint Louis Cardinals. He won the Cy Young Award in 1982 while playing for the Milwaukee Brewers.

Alfred Matthew "Weird Al" Yankovic (October 23, 1959): Comedic singer and songwriter, best known for his musical parodies of mainstream artists such as Michael Jackson or Nirvana.

Tom Yewcic (May 9, 1932): Played in the American Football League from 1961 to 1966 for the Boston Patriots, and baseball in 1957 for the Detroit Tigers.

Appendix 2

Serbian American Websites

- Embassy of the Republic of Serbia: *http://www.serbiaembusa.org/index.php*
- Saint Lazarus Serbian Orthodox Cathedral "Ravanica": *http://ravanica.org/church/*
- Serbica Americana: *http://www.eserbia.org/*
- Serb National Federation: *http://www.snflife.org/default.asp*
- Serbian Orthodox Diocese of New Gracanica/Midwestern America: *http://www.newgracanica.com/menu_eng.html*
- Serb World U.S.A.: *http://www.serbworldusa.com/*
- Tamburitza Association of America: *http://www.tamburitza.org/TAA/index.html*
- University of Michigan Serbian Student Association: *http://www.umich.edu/~srbija/*

Appendix 3

Serbian Recipes

These recipes originally appeared in the 1955 edition of *Serbian Cookery,* compiled by the members of the Sisters of Ravanica Church in Detroit, Michigan. In the foreword, Vlaiko M. Lugonja emphasized the diversity of the Serbian diaspora and the impact of regionalism on the cuisine. While the recipes represented the finer aspects of Serbian cooking, they also illustrated the desire of the women to preserve their ethnic food heritage for future generations. To that end, they converted all measurements to American standards and ingredients.

Chicken Soup (Pileca Chorba)

Cut up into serving portions a 3 lb. chicken which has been well cleaned and washed. Place it in a six-quart soup pot and cover with about five quarts of cold water. Add the following vegetables which have previously been cleaned and prepared: half bunch of celery, 1 bell pepper, 1 green hot pepper, 1 tomato, 1 bay leaf, 1 parsnip, 2 carrots, 2 medium onions cut in half, several stalks of leek. Place on medium flame. Bear in mind that the chorba, or any soup for that matter, should at no time boil vigorously. When the chicken is done, strain the broth and press the vegetables through a sieve back through the broth. Remove the chicken and set aside until serving time.

Add a little parsley leaves finely chopped to the broth and season to taste with salt. Now heat a little oil in frying pan and when quite hot add 1½ Tbs. flour stirring constantly until flour becomes slightly brown. Now add a little paprika and pour immediately into the broth which has remained on a low flame. Allow the broth to cook for another 10–15 minutes and then proceed with the following "finishing" touch. Place 2 eggs yolks in medium bowl with 2 Tbsp. sour cream and beat very well. Pour hot broth with soup ladle over this mixture of yolk and cream stirring same very vigorously with wooden spoon so that it does not curdle. Keep pouring broth and stirring until bowl is about ½ full and then return all of it back into the pot, again stirring while you do so. Remove from flame immediately, adding the chicken. Squeeze lemon into broth until you have acquired a tarter taste. You may serve lemon wedges with your chorba so that guests can do their own seasoning if they wish. (The "zaprshka" or browned flour can be omitted in the preparation of the chicken chorba without losing too much of the delicious flavor).

Paulina Mijatovich

Broiled Meat Links (Cevapcici)

Mix 2 lbs. lean veal and beef which have been ground together with 1 tsp. black pepper and 1 Tbsp. salt. Mix thoroughly. Dip fingers in cold salted water and then shape some of the meat into finger length shapes or like small sausage links. Place meat on a fine wire grill and grill over hot coals, turning once. Or, broil in oven about 10 min. until nicely browned. Serve with finely minced green onions or "ajvar" (eggplant relish).

Irena Shatrich Chapin

Roast Suckling Pig (Peceno Sisance)

The pig should weigh about 16 lbs. Wash it thoroughly and drain. Salt it inside and outside generously. Cut slits under the shoulders and on the thighs. Put 1 tsp. salt and a cut piece of garlic in each slit. Put 6 cloves of garlic and 1 Tbsp. salt in a clean cloth. Pound this slightly with a hammer. Rub cloth over pig inside and outside. Put ½ loaf of unsliced bread inside of pig. In the largest roasting pan, place 2 short pieces of clean board (so the roast won't stick to bottom of pan). Cover top of pig with foil of heavy parchment paper. Place shiny apple in the mouth. Bake at 350° for 5 to 6 hrs. basting with oil once or twice. It is done when no pink juice runs when pierced with fork. Remove bread and dispose of it. Serve hot or cold. If apples become soft after baking, replace with a fresh one.

Draga Jocich

Stuffed Cabbage Rolls (Sarma)

Place a large pan of water on to boil. Add 1 Tbsp. salt. Remove as much core as possible from a head of cabbage. When water boils, put head of cabbage in and cook about 5 min., or until leaves soften. Meat is used and this can vary according to taste: Some use ground ham and pork, others use ground beef and veal mixed. Experiment and determine which you like best. Here is a sample recipe:

1 large onion, chopped
1 clove garlic, minced
1 lb. ground beef
½ lb. ground pork
salt and pepper
6 Tbsp. rice
2 eggs

Fry onions and garlic in hot fat until soft. Add meat and fry until light brown. Remove from heat. Add seasonings and rice. When cooled slightly, add eggs. Mix well. Remove leaves from head of cabbage one at a time. Trim heavy vein on leaf with a sharp knife but don't cut the leaf through. Place 2 Tbsp. of meat filling on the leaf. Roll up and then push ends in firmly. This takes a little practice and if you can't roll them easily the first time, use toothpicks to seal rolls. Put a few scraps and leaves of cabbage on bottom of pan. Then pile rolls neatly on top of this. Fill all leaves with meat until both are used. Canned tomatoes, tomato juice, or tomato soup is then poured over the mixture, whichever is most handy. Then pour 2 cups water or just about enough to cover [rolls]. Cover pan and simmer 1½ hours. Peppers, squash, grape leaves, and tomatoes can be stuffed the same way.

A Friend

Patron Saint's Cake (Slavski Kolac)

Mix egg yolks with sugar until foamy. Add 1 c. heated milk and butter. Cool to lukewarm, add yeast. Let stand until bubbly. Add rest of milk (which has cooled to lukewarm) and part of the flour, and mix very thoroughly. Add rest of the flour and let rise in a warm place covered with a towel. After first rising, turn on board, find a comfortable place, and knead an hour. (This gives the Kolac a wonderful texture.) The last 10 min. of kneading, work in ½ lb. of firm butter in small lumps. When lumps of butter are worked into dough, cut dough into 3 equal parts, putting aside a small amount for trimming. Roll each part into a long piece and braid these 3 pieces together. Place in a large, deep, greased pan and strip and twist. Place this around edge of pan. Make a cross from last of dough and place in center. (Other shapes may be made for trimming, but the twisted edge and cross are compulsory.) Put in warm place (covered with a towel) to rise about 2 hrs. or more. When double in bulk, paint top, except the cross, with beaten egg yolk. The cross should stand out white against the baked glaze. Bake for 2 hrs. at 275°. This is a large Kolac, suitable for Slavas and for use in church.

Saveta Hajdukovich

Traditional Christmas Cake (Cesnica)

Grease a round, deep pie pan. Place three layers strudel dough which is quite dry in the pan with melted butter in between the layers. Sprinkle ground walnuts and a few white raisins on next layers of dough. Continue on in this way until pan is filled with layers. In between top three layers of dough sprinkle melted butter but no nuts or raisins. Trim edges. Press dough down slightly. Place a small glass top down in center of cake. With a sharp knife cut around glass down through the layers to the bottom. Remove glass. Away from this cut circle slip a silver coin in between the layers. Cut diamond-shaped pieces in rest of pie. Pour ½ c. melted butter over all and bake at 350° until golden brown. Meanwhile, prepare a syrup. Cook 1 c. honey with ½ c. water. Pour that hot syrup over the "chesnica" as soon as it is removed from the oven.

Draga Jocich

Notes

1. Michael Palairet, *The Balkan Economies c.1800–1914: Evolution without Development* (London: Cambridge University Press, 1997), 88–89 and 122–123.
2. Steven K. Pavlowitch, *Serbia: The History of an Idea* (New York: New York University Press, 2002), 65.
3. Mirjana Gross, "Social Structure and National Movements among the Yugoslav Peoples on the Eve of the First War," *Slavic Review* 36, no. 4 (December 1977): 631.
4. Vjekoslav Perica, *Balkan Idols: Religion and Nationalism in Yugoslav States* (New York: Oxford University Press, 2002), 123–132.
5. Tim Judah, *The Serbs: History, Myth, and the Destruction of Yugoslavia* (New Haven, CT: Yale University Press, 1997), 3–7.
6. Joel M. Halpern, *A Serbian Village* (New York: Harper Colophon Books, 1967), 36.
7. Ivo Banac, *The National Question in Yugoslavia: Origins, History, Politics* (Ithaca, NY: Cornell University Press, 1984), 69, 76–77.
8. Halpern, *A Serbian Village,* 23–26.
9. Ibid., 54.
10. M. E. Durham, *Some Tribal Origins, Laws, and Customs of the Balkans* (London: George Allen & Unwin Ltd., 1923), 76–80.

11. Christopher Boehm, *Blood Revenge: The Anthropology of Feuding in Montenegro and Other Tribal Societies* (Lawrence: University Press of Kansas, 1984), 165–173.
12. Christopher Boehm, *Montenegrin Social Organization and Values: Political Ethnography of a Refuge Area Tribal Adaptation* (New York: AMS Press, 1983), 32–41.
13. Palairet, *Balkan Economies,* 357–370.
14. Radovan Samardžić, "Migrations in Serbian History," in *Migrations in Balkan History,* ed. Ivan Ninic (Belgrade: Institute of Balkan Studies, 1989), 83–90.
15. F. Clever Bald, *Michigan in Four Centuries* (New York: Harper & Brothers, 1961), 365–368.
16. Ibid., 352.
17. Willis Frederick Dunbar, *Michigan: A History of the Wolverine State* (Grand Rapids: William B. Eerdmans Publishing Co., 1965), 500–503.
18. 1920 United States Census, http://persi.heritagequestonline.com.
19. Josephine Wtulich, *American Xenophobia and the Slav Immigrant: A Living Legacy of Mind and Spirit* (New York: Columbia University Press, 1994), 15.
20. Reports of the Immigration Commission: Statistical Review of Immigration, 1820–1910 (Washington, DC: Government Printing Office, 1911).
21. Reports of the Immigration Commission: Dictionary of Races or Peoples (Washington, DC: Government Printing Office, 1911), 45–51.
22. Jerome Kisslinger, *The Serbian Americans* (New York: Chelsea House Publishers, 1990), 42.
23. Bozidar Dragicevich, "American Serb" (master's thesis, University of Minnesota, 1973), 26.
24. Ivan Cizmic, "Yugoslav Immigrants in the U.S. Labor Movement, 1880–1920," in *American Labor and Immigrant History: Recent European Research,* ed. Dirk Hoerder (Urbana: University of Illinois Press, 1983), 180.
25. June Miljevich Raynal, "Living and Logging: The Miljevich Story," *Serb World* 4, no. 5 (May/June 1988): 40–43.
26. Georgios P. Loizides, "'Making Men' at Ford: Ethnicity, Race, and Americanization during the Progressive Era," *Michigan Sociological Review* 20 (Fall 2007): 109–148, 129–130.
27. Ibid., 128–129.
28. Servian Orthodox Society, St. Michael Archangel Lodge #107 of Calumet, Michigan, Michigan Tech University Archives.
29. Steve Lehto, *Death's Door: The Truth behind Michigan's Largest Mass Murder* (Troy, MI: Momentum Books, 2006), 16–18.

30. Ibid, 146–147.
31. Dragicevich, "American Serb," 72–76.
32. Philip S. Foner, *The Industrial Workers of the World, 1905–1917* (New York: International Publishers, 1965), 383–390.
33. Alex Susnar, "Report of the South Slav Socialist Federation to the National Committee of the Socialist Party of America, May 1913," http://www.marxists.org/history/usa/parties/lfed/southslavic/1913/0500-susnar-reporttonc.pdf.
34. Cizmic, "Yugoslav Immigrants," 188.
35. Dragicevich, "American Serb," 33.
36. Joseph S. Roucek, "The Image of the Slav in U.S. History and Immigrant Policy," *American Journal of Economics and Sociology* 28, no. 1 (January 1969): 29–48, 41–43.
37. Wtulich, *American Xenophobia and the Slav Immigrant,* 44.
38. Joseph S. Roucek, "The Yugoslav Immigrants in America," *American Journal of Sociology* 40, no. 5 (March 1935): 602–611.
39. Gerald Gilbert Govorchin, *Americans from Yugoslavia* (Gainesville: University of Florida Press, 1961), 70–71.
40. Ibid., 280–281.
41. Deborah Padgett, *Settlers and Sojourners: A Study of Serbian Adaptation in Milwaukee, Wisconsin* (New York: AMS Press Inc., 1989).
42. Ibid., 145.
43. Ibid., 146.
44. Ibid., 147–154.
45. Branco Mita Colakovic, *Yugoslav Migration to America* (San Francisco: R + E Research Associates, 1973), 70.
46. Padgett, *Settlers and Sojourners,* 204–211.
47. Michael Ranville, *To Strike at a King: The Turning Point in the McCarthy Witch-Hunts* (Troy, MI: Momentum Books, 1997), 33–35.
48. Ibid., 5.
49. Ibid., 136–140.
50. Ibid., 140–147.
51. Joel M. Halpern, *A Serbian Village,* 140–142.
52. Ibid., 170–175.
53. Ibid., 188–189.
54. Ibid., 192–199.
55. Ibid., 200.

56. Zorka Milich, *A Stranger's Supper: An Oral History of Centenarian Women in Montenegro* (New York: Twayne Publishers, 1995), 23–29.
57. Ibid., 7–10.
58. Ibid., 10–17.
59. Ibid., 19.
60. Kyle E. Ciani, "Hidden Laborers: Female Day Workers in Detroit, 1870-1920," *Journal of the Gilded Age and Progressive Era* 4, no. 1 (January 2005): 23–51, 28.
61. Ibid., 37.
62. Patricia A. Cooper, *Once a Cigar: Men, Women, and Work Culture in American Cigar Factories, 1900–1919* (Chicago: University of Illinois Press), 91–95.
63. "What Price Spinsterhood?," *American Srbobran*, July 27, 1939.
64. Dragicevich, "American Serb," 163–167.
65. "Federation of Serbian Sisters Circles of the Serbian Orthodox Free Church of the United States of America and Canada," http://www.campgracanica.com/ksshistory.pdf.
66. Dragicevich, "American Serb," 163–167.
67. "Serbian Sisters Ravanica," memo, Saint Lazarus Cathedral, Detroit Michigan, Ravanica Church Archive.
68. Protinica Paulina Mijatovich, "75th Anniversary of the Parish of St. Lazarus Serbian Orthodox Church Ravanica, October 13–14, 1990," Ravanica Church Archive.
69. "Serbian Sisters Ravanica," memo.
70. "Federation of Serbian Sisters Circles of the Serbian Orthodox Free Church of the United States of America and Canada," http://www.campgracanica.com/ksshistory.pdf.
71. "Serbian Sisters Ravanica," memo.
72. "Kuma Writes," *Diocesan Observer*, September 29, 1965; and "KSS: Right Arm of Church," *Diocesan Observer*, December 1, 1965.
73. Padgett, *Settlers and Sojourners*, 78.
74. "Our Great Patron Kuma Anja Dead," *Diocesan Observer*, February 11, 1970.
75. "Kuma's Gift of KSS Home to Us," *Diocesan Observer*, September 3, 1969.
76. "Funeral at L.A.," *Diocesan Observer*, February 18, 1970.
77. "Serbian Sisters Ravanica," memo.
78. "Detroit Serb Women's Club $22,000," *American Srbobran*, November 10, 1971.
79. Cathedral of St. Sava, http://www.hramsvetogsave.com/Hram/ser/Vesti/default.htm.

80. Mildred Radjenovic, *Cook Book: Circle of Serbian Sisters* (Milwaukee: Hammersmith-Breithaupt Printing Co., 1973), 14.
81. Zora D. Zimmerman, "Traditions and Change in a Ritual Feast: The Serbian Krsna Slava in America," *Great Lakes Review* 11, no. 2 (Fall 1985): 21–36.
82. Stanimir Spasovic, *The History of the Serbian Orthodox Church in America and Canada, 1941–1991* (Belgrade: Printing House of the Serbian Patriarchate, 1998), 283–284.
83. Stan Carlson and the Very Rev. Leonid Soroka, *Faith of Our Fathers: The Eastern Orthodox Religion* (Minneapolis: Olympic Press, 1958), 74–81.
84. Sisters of Ravanica, *Serbian Cookery* (Ann Arbor: Braun-Brumfield, 1955), 130–131.
85. Ibid., 129.
86. Dragicevich, "American Serb," 86.
87. Sisters of Ravanica, *Serbian Cookery,* 129.
88. Mijatovich, "75th Anniversary."
89. Padgett, *Settlers and Sojourners,* 203.
90. "How to Organize English Speaking Lodges," *American Srbobran,* August 29, 1937.
91. Stanimir Spasovic, *The History of the Serbian Orthodox Church in America and Canada, 1941–1991* (Belgrade: Printing House of the Serbian Patriarchate, 1998), 56–57.
92. "Petition Explains Conditions in Serbia," *American Serb* 2, no. 2 (February 1945).
93. "Partisan Prisoner Tells of Massacre of Intellectuals," *American Serb* 2, no. 7 (December 1945).
94. Mijatovich, "75th Anniversary," 7.
95. "Detroit Rebuilds," *American Serb Life* 1, no. 4 (May 1948).
96. Spasovic, *History of the Serbian Orthodox Church,* 85–90.
97. Djuro J. Vrga, "Differential Associational Involvement of Successive Ethnic Immigrations: An Indicator of Ethno-Religious Factionalism and Alienation of Immigrants," *Social Forces* 50, no. 2 (December 1971): 239–248.
98. "Our Struggle for Freedom: History of the Serbian Orthodox Dispute," Immigrant History Research Center, University of Minnesota. http://www.ihrc.umn.edu/
99. Padgett, *Settlers and Sojourners,* 165.
100. "Our Struggle for Freedom: History of the Serbian Orthodox Dispute," Immigrant History Research Center.

101. “Appeals Court Ruling—What They Mean,” *Diocesan Observer,* April 20, 1966.
102. “Diocese Stands by Its Bishops, Ousts Rebels,” *Diocesan Observer,* May 11, 1966.
103. “A Monumental Fraud,” *Diocesan Observer,* December 20, 1966.
104. Dragicevich, “American Serb,” 108–120.
105. Spasovic, *History of the Serbian Orthodox Church,* 216.
106. Ibid., 199.
107. Ibid., 228–229.
108. “Our Church Up North,” *Diocesan Observer,* December 6, 1967.
109. “Detroit Land Rites,” *Diocesan Observer,* September 22, 1965.
110. “Detroit Blessing,” *Diocesan Observer,* September 12, 1967.
111. “Glory and Agony Alike,” *Diocesan Observer,* December 8, 1965.
112. “Singer Pilgrimage to Titoland . . . For What?,” *Diocesan Observer,* February 16, 1966.
113. “Loyalty to Whom—LBJ or German—Tito,” *Diocesan Observer,* March 27, 1968.
114. Spasovic, *History of the Serbian Orthodox Church,* 333–335.
115. “Resolution of the Second Diocesan Church—People Assembling,” *Diocesan Observer,* November 15, 1981.
116. Spasovic, *History of the Serbian Orthodox Church,* 338–340.
117. Dragicevich, “American Serb,” 20.
118. Celia Hawkesworth, *Voice in the Shadows: Women and Verbal Art in Serbia and Bosnia* (Budapest: Central European University Press, 2000), 24–25.
119. Margaret Schmidt, “Ugly Music: Learning to Listen Respectfully,” *General Music Today* 25, no. 1 (October 2011): 8–13.
120. Mark Levy, “Southeastern European (Balkan) Music,” in *The Garland Encyclopedia of World Music: The United States and Canada,* ed. Ellen Koskoff (New York: Garland Publishing, Inc., 2001), 919–924.
121. Peter M. Fekula, “Assimilation Works Both Ways,” *American Srbobran,* October 14, 1937.
122. Levy, “Southeastern European (Balkan) Music,” 919–924.
123. Milan Opacich, *Tamburitza America* (Tucson: Black Mountain Publishers, 2005), 75–84.
124. Sarena Tamburitza Orchestra, http://www.sarenaorchestra.com/.
125. Opacich, *Tamburitza America,* 172.
126. John Milich, “She Stands Alone,” in *Serb World U.S.A.* (Tucson: Black Mountain Publishers, July and August 1987), 41–43.
127. Opacich, *Tamburitza America,* 172–173.

128. Levy, "Southeastern European (Balkan) Music," 919–924.
129. Inja Stanic, "The Influences of Yugoslav Folklore on Two Contemporary Balkan Composers: Vojin Komadina and Ivan Jevtic," *Perspectives of New Music* 35, no. 2 (Summer 1997): 137–179.
130. Opacich, *Tamburitza America,* 228–231.
131. Levy, "Southeastern European (Balkan) Music," 919–924.
132. "Vladimir M. Lugonja, 1898–1977: Founder, Serbian Singing Federation," Ravanica Church Archive.
133. Kisslinger, *The Serbian Americans,* 85–89.
134. "Serbian Singing Federation," Ravanica Church Archive.
135. Serbian Singing Federation, http://www.serbiansingingfederation.org/.

For Further Reference

Anzulovic, Branimir. *Heavenly Serbia: From Myth to Genocide.* New York: New York University Press, 1999.

Balch, Emily G. *Our Slavic Fellow Citizens.* New York: Charities Publication Committee, 1910.

Banac, Ivo. *The National Question in Yugoslavia: Origins, History, Politics.* Ithaca, NY: Cornell University Press, 1984.

Bodnar, John E. *Immigration and Industrialization: Ethnicity in an American Milltown, 1870–1940.* Pittsburgh, PA: University of Pittsburgh Press, 1977.

———. *The Transplanted: A History of Immigrants in Urban America.* Bloomington: University of Indiana Press, 1985.

———. *Workers' World: Kinship, Community, and Protest in an Industrial Society, 1900–1940.* Baltimore: Johns Hopkins University Press, 1982.

Boehm, Christopher. *Blood Revenge: The Anthropology of Feuding in Montenegro and Other Tribal Societies.* Lawrence: University Press of Kansas, 1984.

———. *Montenegrin Social Organization and Values: Political Ethnography of a Refuge Area Tribal Adaptation.* New York: AMS Press, 1983.

Cetinich, Daniel. *South Slavs in Michigan.* East Lansing: Michigan State University Press, 2003.

Ciani, Kyle E. "Hidden Laborers: Female Day Workers in Detroit, 1870–1920." *Journal of the Gilded Age and Progressive Era* 4, no. 1 (2005).

Cizmic, Ivan. "Yugoslav Immigrants in the U.S. Labor Movement, 1880–1920." In *American Labor and Immigrant History, 1877–1920: Recent European Research*, ed. Dirk Hoerder. Urbana: University of Illinois Press, 1983.

Cooper, Patricia A. *Once a Cigar: Men, Women, and Work Culture in American Cigar Factories, 1900–1919*. Chicago: University of Illinois Press, 1987.

Davies, E. Chivers. *Tales of Serbian Life*. London: George G. Harrap & Co., 1919.

Dragicevich, Bozidar. "American Serb." Master's thesis, University of Minnesota, 1973.

Dragnich, Alex N. *Serbia and Yugoslavia: Historical Studies and Contemporary Commentaries*. New York: Columbia University Press, 1998.

Dragnich, Alex N., and Slavco Todorovich. *The Saga of Kosovo: Focus on Serbian-Albanian Relations*. New York: Columbia University Press, 1984.

Dragović-Soso, Jana. *Saviours of the Nation: Serbia's Intellectual Opposition and the Revival of Nationalism*. Montreal: McGill-Queen's University Press, 2002.

Durham, M. E. *Some Tribal Origins, Laws, and Customs of the Balkans*. London: George Allen & Unwin Ltd., 1923.

Foner, Philip S. *The Industrial Workers of the World, 1905–1917*. New York: International Publishers, 1965.

Gagnon, V. P., Jr. *The Myth of Ethnic War: Serbia and Croatia in the 1990s*. Ithaca, NY: Cornell University Press, 2004.

Gallager, Tom, ed. *The Balkans in the New Millennium: In the Shadow of War and Peace*. New York: Routledge, Taylor & Francis Group, 2005.

Glenny, Misha. *The Balkans: Nationalism, War, and the Great Powers, 1804–1999*. New York: Penguin Books, 1999.

Gordy, Eric D. *The Culture of Power in Serbia: Nationalism and the Destruction of Alternatives*. University Park: Pennsylvania State University Press, 1999.

Govorchin, Gerald. *Americans from Yugoslavia*. Gainesville: University of Florida Press, 1961.

Gross, Mirjana. "Social Structure and National Movements among the Yugoslav Peoples on the Eve of the First War." *Slavic Review* 36, no. 4 (1977).

Halpern, Joel M. *A Serbian Village*. New York: Harper Colophon Books, 1967.

Hawkesworth, Celia. *Voices in the Shadows: Women and Verbal Art in Serbia and Bosnia*. Budapest: Central European University Press, 2000.

Held, Joseph. *The Columbia History of Eastern Europe in the Twentieth Century*. New York: Columbia University Press, 1992.

Hupchick, Dennis P. *The Balkans: From Constantinople to Communism*. New York:

Palgrave Macmillan, 2002.

Jelavich, Charles, and Barbara Jelavich. *The Establishment of the Balkan National States, 1804–1920.* Seattle: University of Washington Press, 1977.

Judah, Tim. *The Serbs: History, Myth, and the Destruction of Yugoslavia.* New Haven, CT: Yale University Press, 1997.

Kaplan, Robert D. *Balkan Ghosts: A Journey through History.* New York: St. Martin's Press, 1993.

Kisslinger, Jerome. *The Serbian Americans.* New York: Chelsea House Publishers, 1990.

Lehto, Steve. *Death's Door: The Truth behind Michigan's Largest Mass Murder.* Troy, MI: Momentum Books, 2006.

Loizides, Georgios P. "'Making Men' at Ford: Ethnicity, Race, and Americanization during the Progressive Era." *Michigan Sociological Review* 20 (Fall 2007).

Low, D. H., trans. *The Ballads of Marko Kraljevi⊠.* New York: Greenwood Press, 1968.

Mazower, Mark. *The Balkans: A Short History.* New York: Modern Library, 2002.

Mijatovies, Csedomille, trans. *Serbian Folk-Lore.* New York: Benjamin Blom Inc., 1968.

Milich, Zorka. *A Stranger's Supper: An Oral History of Centenarian Women in Montenegro.* New York: Twayne Publishers, 1995.

Miyatovic, Elodie L. *Serbian Fairy Tales.* London: William Heinemann, 1917.

Mugge, Maximilian A. *Serbian Folk Songs, Fairy Tales and Proverbs.* London: Drane's Danegeld House, 1916.

Norris, David A. *Belgrade: A Cultural History.* New York: Oxford University Press, 2009.

Opacich, Milan. *Tamburitza America.* Tucson: Black Mountain Publishers, 2005.

Padgett, Deborah. *Settlers and Sojourners: A Study of Serbian Adaptation in Milwaukee, Wisconsin.* New York: AMS Press Inc., 1989.

Palairet, Michael. *The Balkan Economies c.1800–1914: Evolution without Development.* London: Cambridge University Press, 1997.

Pavlowitch, Steven K. *Serbia: The History of an Idea.* New York: New York University Press, 2002.

Perica, Vjekoslav. *Balkan Idols: Religion and Nationalism in Yugoslav States.* New York: Oxford University Press, 2002.

Petrovich, Michael B., and Joel Halpern. "Serbs." In *Harvard Encyclopedia of American Ethnic Groups,* ed. Stephan Thernstrom, Ann Orlov, and Oscar Handlin, 916–26. Cambridge, MA: Belknap Press of Harvard University Press, 1980.

Ranville, Michael. *To Strike at a King: The Turning Point in the McCarthy Witch-Hunts.* Troy, MI: Momentum Books, 1997.

Raynal, June Miljevich. "Living and Logging: The Miljevich Story." *Serb World* 4, no. 5 (1988).

Samardžić, Radovan. "Migrations in Serbian History." In *Migrations in Balkan History,* ed. Ivan Ninic. Belgrade: Institute of Balkan Studies, 1989.

Thomas, Robert. *The Politics of Serbia in the 1990s.* New York: Columbia University Press, 1999.

"What Price Spinsterhood?," *American Srbobran,* July 27, 1939.

Wtulich, Josephine. *American Xenophobia and the Slav Immigrant: A Living Legacy of Mind and Spirit.* New York: Columbia University Press, 1994.

Index

C

D

M

N

O

P

R

S